I0478607

# CPA - Formation One

# ACCA – F4

# ATI Law and Ethics

# Business Laws and Professional Ethics

**Teresa Clyne BA, MSc**

# CPA/ACCA/ATI - BUSINESS LAW CRAM NOTES

## Introduction

Welcome to my ATI / ACCA / CPA law notes booklet, before I go on, I will just explain that not every topic in the ATI / ACCA / CPA exams is covered in this book but probably 70% of the major areas are, (**this is a revision and cram booklet, not a textbook**).   I teach ATI & CPA law and ethics and business management and have found that putting notes together for my students has proved invaluable and also helps me to ensure that no areas are left unstudied.

The primary aim of law revision is to prepare yourself for the exams ahead, these law notes have all of the relevant topics you need to pass your ATI / ACCA / CPA exam, of course you must have the information in the first place so ensure you have bought a good law manual, (**my business law book, which covers ALL of the** ATI / ACCA / CPA **modules and LO's, An Introduction to Business Law is available on Amazon**)

It is vital that you prepare your study time using a study planner, (laid out below). Type or rewrite your lecture or book notes, (do not highlight) you learn easier and quicker when you are writing the notes, ensure that you use your textbook alongside your notes; this ensures you go back to cases etc. (I have not put many cases in these notes, these are notes not executive summaries)

Leave room in your notes for addendums and highlight those, use as little highlighting as possible, this ensure that your brain focuses on the highlights not merely sweeping by a whole page of highlights.

Doodle, yes doodle, draw little reminders, draw aspects which you can easily remember, use word association such as in the law of contract one case which dealt with the illegal sale of **birds**, was **Partridge** v Crittenden, *a partridge is a bird....*

Case names are very important, however it is just as important to know the facts of the case, and the ruling in the case, so I would suggest you read as many articles (and your textbooks) on each case, do your own notes and addendums, and be sure to write down the ruling.

Learning law is like learning a new language, so understand that you need to be immersed in it, to grasp it, read as many legal articles as you can, legal journals, find areas of law which really interest you. And my number one numer ono, numer jeden, get out and have some fun, it is okay to have a life, to have fun, hang out with your friends, just remember that all work and no play makes.......

## Time your revision

20 or 30 minute stretches are the most productive when revising, spending hours without a break is counterproductive.

The times below are only examples and module are also examples, the important thing is you ensure that you have proper rest breaks, drink plenty of water, and take fish oils, if you don't like fresh oily fish then get some oils, this will ensure that your brain is at its optimal performance.

### Study schedule (example)

9.00-9.30 LO1 (module one and two)
Break 5 mins
9.35-10.05 LO2 (module two)
Break 5 mins
10.10-10.40 LO1 (module three)
Break 5 mins
10.45-11.15 LO3 (module one)
Break 30 mins
11.45-12.15 LO4 (module two)
Break 5 mins
12.20-12.50 LO5 (module one and two)
Break 1 hour
13.50-14.20 LO6 (module three)
Break 5 mins
14.25-14.55 LO5 (module three)
Break 5 mins
15.00-15.30 LO7 (module two and three)
Break 5 mins
15.35-16.05 LO7 (module one)

Disclaimer: while every effort is made to ensure the accuracy of the information contained in this booklet, Teresa Clyne accepts no responsibility for any errors therein, nor does she take any responsibility for any student's reliance on the enclosed notes. N.B. ***this is a revision and cram booklet, not a textbook***

## Hints and Tips on answering your Multiple Choice Questions in your exams

The questions in your exam will each contain four possible answers. You have to choose the option that best answers the question. The three incorrect options are called distractors. There is a skill in answering MCQs quickly and correctly. By practising MCQs you can develop this skill, giving you a better chance of passing the exam.

You may wish to follow the approach outlined below, or you may prefer to adapt it.

**Step 1;** Attempt each question. Read the question thoroughly. You may prefer to work out the answer before looking at the options, or you may prefer to look at the options at the beginning. Adopt the method that works best for you.

**Step 2;** Read the four options and see if one matches your own answer. Be careful with numerical questions, as the distractors are designed to match answers that incorporate common errors.

**Step 3**; you may find that none of the options matches your answer.

*   Re-read the question to ensure that you understand it and are answering the requirement
*   Eliminate any obviously wrong answers
*   Consider which of the remaining answers is the most likely to be correct and select the option

**Step 4**; if you are still unsure make a note and continue to the next question. Some questions will take you longer to answer than others. Try to reduce the average time per question, to allow yourself to revisit problem questions at the end of the exam.

**Step 5**; Revisit unanswered questions. When you come back to a question after a break you often find you are able to answer it correctly straight away. If you are still unsure have a guess. You are not penalised for incorrect answers, so never leave a question unanswered!

# CPA/ACCA/ATI - BUSINESS LAW CRAM NOTES

## Table of Contents

## Section One – LO1 – The Irish Legal System

### The Organs of State

Ireland has a **tripartite separation of powers**; this means there are **three** branches or **organs** of state.  Each branch is responsible for different parts of running the country. Each one is **independent of each other** and no one **Organ of State** can interfere or make decisions on behalf of another.

- ➡ **the legislature** (*Oireachtas/Parliament "all parties in the Dáil"*), this is the overall parties in the Dáil, the legislature consists of two houses; Dáil Éireann (House of Representatives) and Seanad Éireann (the Senate) plus the president, plus all political parties and independent ministers. All Bills must be passed by each House and be signed into law by the President.

- ➡ **the executive** (*government "the party in power")*, they have control of the day to day running of the Oireachtas or the Parliament.  They are elected officials.  They comprise of the Taoiseach (president) and the Tánaiste (vice president)

- ➡ **the judiciary** (the courts), judges ensure the correct interpretation of the laws passed by the legislative branch and enforced by the executive branch.

### Separation of Powers

*"Power tends to corrupt, and absolute power corrupts absolutely. Great men are almost always bad men."* John Emerich Edward Dalberg Acton (**Lord Acton**)

The concept of the 'rule of law' is closely bound up with that of the **separation of powers**. Most clearly democratic nations in the world have power held in different places, so that no part of the political process holds too much influence. They usually have:
1. An elected **legislature**, (The Oireachtas/Dáil) a body which decides on what laws should be passed to ensure that the people's wishes – for example, freedom or wealth – are met.
2. An elected **executive**, or government body, (The Current government is a fine Gael, fianna fail coalition), which makes the decisions that put the laws into action.

3. A **judiciary**, (Judges/courts), rules on any disputes about laws, whether between the government and the people (**criminal law**) or between individuals (**civil law**).

In Ireland the **legislature**, the **executive** and the **judiciary** are completely separate, therefore each is accountable to, and can operate as a *'check and balance'* on, the others, however there is a **complex relationship** between the three sets of powers. This means that a balance is struck between control and accountability, on the one hand, and actually 'getting things did' on the other.

### The Attorney General

The Attorney General of Ireland, also referred to as the AG is the principal legal adviser to the Irish Government.    The Attorney- General's office incorporates
- Chief State Solicitor's office
- The Office of Parliamentary Counsel
- The Statute Law Revision Unit

The AG's powers and responsibilities encompass the following:
- The AG scrutinises all draft legislation Under Article 30 of the Irish Constitution:
- The AG is the adviser of the Government in matters of law and legal opinion'.
- The AG advises the Government on international law and extradition requests
- Defendant in constitutional challenges
- They can give advice to the government and perform all legal duties on all legal matters.
- The AG is appointed by Taoiseach

### The Director of Public Prosecutions

The Law Officers of Ireland: The Director of Public Prosecutions is also known as the DPP.

Under **Article 30** of the Irish Constitution, the DPP;
- enforces criminal law on behalf of the people of Ireland
- directs/supervises public prosecutions on indictment
- direction and advice to the Gardaí on summary cases
- they are appointed by Government, but they are Civil Servants.

## The Rule of Law

**The rule of law** states that all people are **equal** under the **law**. **No one is above the law**, whether they are a politician, a Garda, a Judge, corporation or wealthy individual. The courts exist to ensure that **everyone** is accountable to the **law**

## Sources of law in Ireland

- **The Irish Constitution:** Bunreacht na hÉireann, 1937
- **Statute Law,** subject to interpretation by the courts, and must be Constitutional
- **Case Law and Precedent** / **Common law,** previous binding decisions of courts in cases which are reported in the law reports
- **EU Law**, primary legislation, supreme to national law.

## Bunreacht na hÉireann, 1937

The Primary source of law in Ireland prior to joining the EU. The Constitution is a positive source of rights for Irish citizens, it confirms that the State is obliged to protect citizen's rights; this is done by enacting legislation if necessary. All other sources must be "constitutional" otherwise it will be repugnant to the Irish state and can be challenged before the courts. *Crotty V An Taoiseach (1987)*

## Common law (Case Law and Precedent)

The decisions of judges in previous cases are binding on lower courts. Built up from the Common Customs & Precedents. This principle is called 'Stare Decisis' . This means literally 'to stand by what has been decided' and it is at the heart of the doctrine of precedent.

The **obiter is NOT** binding, but it is persuasive (taken into consideration). (*obiter, 'things said by the way'*)

**Ratio decidendi** - the reason for the decision
Defined as '*any rule expressly or impliedly treated by the judge as a necessary step in reaching his conclusion*'.

The **ratio IS binding** on all lower courts
Courts at a lower or similar level must follow precedent – unless the court can distinguish, as in *AG v Ryans Car Hire 1965*

***Persuasive precedent*** is precedent taken from, for example, another country, or a lower court; it is never binding how the judge makes take it into consideration when reaching his decision...

The main difference between Case law & Precedent AND Legislation is:
Case law is retrospective, it looks back on previous decision to make a decision in the present case, and it also looks forward to other similar cases. Legislation looks forward, the legislation or the instruction contained in the act are to ensure present and future adherence to the will of the Oireachtas.

## Legislation

## Primary legislation

Primary legislation is an Act of the Oireachtas which passes the five stages of a Bill (the bill is introduced by either private members or public members bill, goes to the Oireachtas/Dáil, to the Seanad and is passed into law, if the Seanad do not pass the Bill the Dáil can refer it back to itself in 90 days and pass without the Seanad) and is signed into law by the President, the President may, under Article 26 of the Constitution refer a Bill to the Supreme Court for Clarification.

## Secondary/delegated legislation

In order not to overload the Oireachtas the Government can confer (give) powers to a minister or body in the Primary Act to make delegated/subordinated/secondary legislation, delegated legislation such as statutory instruments, may be used for example to uprate certain annual grants and benefits where the basic rules have been agreed in primary legislation but the rates or amounts need to be altered from time to time.(i.e., fines, penalty points etc.) this means that a full life of a bill and legislation though all the stages of the Oireachtas and Seanad is not necessary.

There are five main types of statutory instrument orders, regulations, rules, bye-laws and schemes.

Example of an **Order**: *The Road Traffic Act 2004* (*primary act*) The Manager of a City or County Council can reduce the speed limit on a road undergoing road works for a stated period of time by executive order under powers available to him/her under the *Road Traffic Act 2004*: ***Road Traffic (Speed Limits) (County Borough of Dublin and County of Dublin) (Amendment) Regulations, 1992***. (This means local speed limits, i.e. road works or certain bad areas "*on the n52, there are 80 and 100km limits as the roads* *are so bad in some places"* can be changed without having to change the WHOLE ACT.)

## Avoiding / Departing from precedent

### *Overruling*

This is where a court higher in the hierarchy departs from a decision made in a lower court. The previous decision is no longer binding.

### *Reversing*

This is where a higher court departs from the decision of the lower court on appeal.

### *Distinguishing*

This is where the facts of the case are deemed sufficiently different so that the previous case is no longer binding.

Also:

The Ratio is obscure or unclear
The Precedent cited is too broad
The Precedent is in conflict with principle of law
In curiam – lack of care
Sub silentio – precedent was decided on point of law not argued in court

## Statutory Interpretation

### *Literal Rule:*

Applying plain, ordinary meanings of the act, reading it straight from the legislation, this is the first to be used by judges, if it results in and absurd result the judges go on to the:

### *Golden Rule:*

Identifying the multiple **meanings of statutory terms** and applying the one which produces a fair and just results, **for example**: *the Offences Against the Person Act 1861 provided that 'whosoever being married shall marry another person during the life of the former husband or wife' is guilty of bigamy",* this wording is ambiguous, as it is impossible to marry while *"already married"* and former, implies they are no longer married. Even though contradictory, the intention of the courts here was to stop people who are already married to marry again. If this also results in an absurd result, the judge will go onto the:

### *Mischief Rule:*

This rule can be used when the judges look to see why the act was passed in the first place, it will seek to assess if a mistake was made in the legislation, what they left out when writing the act itself, **for example:** if an act is passed to stop *"solicitation in the street"* and a person went to **the home** of a person, then they are not in the "street", the reason this act was introduced was to keep the streets clean, so the act did not have going to the door in it, but it can be defined under the mischief rule to have intended this, and the reason for its introduction used in this case. *Smith v. Hughes*

### *Purposive Approach:*

Identifying the purpose of the statute and applying a meaning which enforces that purpose, why was the act made in the first place? Here the judge may define what the act makers intended when making the act, and carry that intention out.

**Ejusdem Generis rule** = same kind or nature = i.e. cows, sheep and goats are **livestock**

### Precedent - authoritative / persuasive

- authoritative precedents is binding precedent,
- persuasive is considered from other jurisdictions, i.e. high court judge **considering** a precedent from the district court, or even from another country.

## Burden of Proof

The burden of proof is the onus of proving the case, i.e. in a criminal case the burden of proof lies with the DPP or the prosecution, in a civil case the burden is on the person bringing the case in litigation, and for instance in a unfair dismissals case the burden of proof lies with the employer, to prove that unfair dismissal did NOT occur, HOWEVER, in constructive dismissal the burden of proof lies with the employee.

## Standard of Proof

The standard of proof is the extent as to the proof required to prove guilt (criminal case) liability (civil case). In a criminal case the standard of proof is BEYOND REASONABLE DOUBT, and in a civil case the standard of proof is ON THE BALANCE OF PROBABILITIES.

## Distinction between criminal and civil cases

It is not an act or event which creates the distinction between criminal and civil cases, but the legal consequences. A single event might give rise to criminal and civil proceedings.

A broken leg caused to a pedestrian by a drunken driver is a single event which may give rise to:
1. A criminal case – prosecution by the State for the offence of driving with excess alcohol, and
2. A civil case – the pedestrian sues for compensation for pain and suffering.

The two sorts of proceedings are usually easily distinguished because three vital factors are different:
1. The courts where the case is heard
2. The procedures.
3. The terminology.

In criminal cases the rules of evidence are usually very strict. For example, a confession will be carefully examined to see if any pressure was brought to bear upon the accused. An admission in a civil case will not usually be subjected to such scrutiny.

## Law of Equity

Equity is a set of maxims, *"rule of thumb"* (*how it's done around here*)

- The courts of equity operate primarily in personam, attacking and binding the conscience of a person.
- Equity looks regards as done which ought to have been done.
- Equity will not suffer a wrong without a remedy.
- Equality is equity.
- Equity regards substance rather than form
- Equity looks to the intention rather the form
- Where the equities are equal, the first in time will prevail.
- Where equities are equal, the law will prevail.
- Equity follows the law.
- He who seeks equity must do equity.

## Equitable remedies can be awarded by a judge when money will not satisfy

Equitable remedies are at the discretion of the court, no legal entitlement to them.  Examples of equitable remedies

- **Injunction;** mandatory, prohibitory, mariva
- **Specific performance** (do the job as specified); (the courts will not grant this where, there is employee contract, where the court has to supervise, seeking to enforce the paying of deposits, against minors, or where it is unfair or unjust to order it)
- **Rectification**; the contract rectified (changed) to give effect to the intention of the parties
- **Recession;** setting the contract aside (it never existed)

## The Commercial Court

- A division of the High Court,  which was established in 2004
- Disputes of a commercial nature where the value of the claim is at least €1 million
- Proceedings under the Arbitration Act 2010 with a value of at least €1 million
- Disputes concerning intellectual property including tort of passing-off

**Courts structure and jurisdiction** of each... *(below)*

# THE STRUCTURE OF IRISH COURTS

The Courts and Court Officers (Amendment) Act 2007 states the numbers of judges in the District court, 63, Circuit, 37, High 37, Special, 11 (from a panel), 3, 5 or 7 in the Supreme Court.

There are other administrative courts such as the Employment Appeals Tribunal, An Bord Pleanála, and the Labour Court inside the court hierarchy and structure.

## Supreme Court

Final Court of Appeal (in cases of Fact only) only hears appeals, this court is not a court of first instance, (it never hears a case for the first time). It deals with matters of law or procedure where it's of national interest for the country such as the constitutionality of any legislation which may be referred under Article 26 of the constitution. The Supreme Court can determine or question capacity of the President. Three (ordinarily) or five (national importance) or 7 (Article 26) judges sit. Decisions made based on majority ruling, although each judge is eligible to provide a separate judgement, whether or not it agrees with majority rulings.

## Court of Criminal Appeal

This court deals with appeals, persons convicted on impeachment in Circuit Court, Central Criminal Court or Special Criminal Court.

## Special Criminal Court

This court deals with criminal charges relating to terrorist organizations and organized drug activities. Brought into being to secure effective administration of justice, preservation of public peace. It consists of three judges sitting without a jury. Set up under the *Offences against the State Act 1939*

## Central Criminal Court

The Central Criminal Court is the criminal section of the High Court, it deals with serious indictable offences,. these would include rape, murder, piracy and treason.

## Court of Civil Appeal

Hears appeals from High Court except cases where Supreme Court permits appeals. Gives ruling on question of law acquiesced to it by, Circuit Courts. It hears appeals from cases heard in High Court about whether or not a law is constitutional.

## High Court

The High Court has *full original jurisdiction (it can hear any case from anywhere for any amount)* in authority to determine, all complications, whether law or fact, civil and criminal. It has the authority to determine the validity of any law which is referred to it from the president under Article 26 of the constitution. It also deals with separation and divorce cases.

## Circuit Court

The Circuit Civil Court deals with cases from €15k to €75k (Contract) and €60k (Tort) it also deals with family law separations and divorce.

The circuit criminal court deals with indictable offences which are less serious, i. e. theft burglary robbery, some less indictable offences can be tried summarily in the district court with permission from the accused, DPP and the Judge. In criminal cases the judge sits with a jury. This court can also hear appeals from the District Court

*Jurisdiction means:* what the court has the power to deal with. i.e limited jurisdiction in the district court is €15,000. Local jurisdiction in the district civil court is where the defendant lives or where the tort or contract took place. Original jurisdiction means a case from any area for any amount.

## Commercial Court

Provides efficient, effective dispute resolution in commercial cases greater than €1 million. Disputes concern of large commercial properties. Appeals or application for judicial review of regulator decisions.

## District Court

The district civil court deals with minor civil law cases, maintenance orders up to €150.00, minor tort cases, this judge has the jurisdiction to deal with cases up to €15,000. this court deals with appeals from employment tribunals.

The district criminal court deals with minor offences, and offences which will give minor fines, in the district court you the maximum fine is €1905 and you will get a maximum sentence of 12 months for one offence and 24 months for two or more offences. This court deals with summary offences (less serious). Judge, no jury.

## Small Claims

Claims up to €2k are dealt with without the need for a solicitor. The District Court Registrar will process the Claim S/he will try to reach a settlement if this is not possible it will be brought before the District Court

*A summary offence* is a minor offence heard by a judge only. Indictable is a more serious offence which is heard by judge and jury.

### *Appeals court structure*

**<u>District Court to the Circuit Court</u>**, (civil to civil, criminal to criminal), circuit to high or appeals, circuit or central criminal to the criminal appeals, (criminal appeals on point of law only to the Supreme)

### Limited Jurisdiction of the district criminal court

Drink driving, TV licence, speeding and parking all dealt with in the district court.

### EU Law, institutions – powers.

### Primary Law

Treaties are the starting point for EU law and are known in the EU as primary law.

### Secondary Law

The body of law that comes from the principles and objectives of the treaties is known as secondary law; and includes regulations, directives, decisions, recommendations and opinions.

### The EU institutions:

The European Council: its main purpose is to stand for the interests of the various economic and social groupings of civil society (ex. employers, workers, farmers, liberal professions, etc.)
The Council of the European Union (also "the Council"):
The European Commission
The European Parliament
The Court of Justice of the European Union
The Court of Auditors
The European Central Bank

**EU Parliament** – Currently 785 MEPs. Based in France, Belgium and Luxembourg (members elected from their own countries).
Passes laws, monitors budget, monitors EU institutions

**EU Council** – Ministerial representations from each member state.
Passes laws, approves EU budget, co-ordination of economic policies, develops foreign policy, co-ordinates anti-crime strategies

**EU Commission** – 20 Commissioners appointed by each member state every 5 years

> (representatives are in their positions due to their expertise and qualifications).
> Proposes legislation, implements EU policies, law enforcement, international coordination.

**Court of Justice** – one judge from each member state

> Interprets and applies EU legislation

## EU Treaties

> **1957 Treaty of Rome**
> **1972 Treaty of Accession -Brussels**
> **1987 Single European Act**
> **1993 Maastricht Treaty (Treaty on European Union)**
> **1997 Treaty of Amsterdam**
> **2003 Nice Treaty**
> **2009 Lisbon Treaty (Treaty of the Functioning of the EU)**
> **2012 European Fiscal Compact Treaty**

## Regulations

A "regulation" is a binding legislative act. It must be applied in its entirety across the EU from the day of enactment, should there be a contradiction between EU and National law, EU is supreme. Regulations are;

- directly applicable
- binding in entirety

## Directives

A "directive" is a legislative act that sets out a goal that all EU countries must achieve. However, it is up to the individual countries how they bring this about. The State must pass National laws to give effect to the requirements in the directive.

## Decisions

A "decision" is binding on those to whom it is addressed

## Recommendations

A "recommendation" is not binding. A recommendation allows the institutions to make their views known and to suggest a line of action without imposing any legal obligation.

## Opinions

An "Opinion" has no binding force. Opinions are not binding, but express the Councils or Commission's view on policy

## The Differences between a solicitor and a barrister in Irish law

- Barristers present legal cases in Court before Judges and Juries as well as give their opinions on questions of law.
- Barristers in Ireland can only act when a solicitor briefs them on a case. They cannot simply turn up in Court and have a right of audience (advocate on behalf of anyone)
- A Solicitor will deal with the client and prepare the case for the barrister to present. (as they have specialised knowledge in that specific area)
- Solicitors can advertise, Barristers cannot.
- Solicitors can form firms, Barristers can come together with other barristers under one roof called a chambers,
- Barristers are self-employed. solicitors are not. They are employed or partners in firms.
- Barristers in the same chamber can work opposing cases, solicitors in the same firm cannot represent two side of a dispute, and this is conflict of interest.
- Solicitors deal directly with the public and contracted to them; barristers are contracted to the solicitor.
- Barristers are specialising in set areas of law, solicitors are knowledgeable in many broad areas of law.
- Solicitors Qualify with the Law Society of Ireland and Barristers qualify with the King's Inn.
- Barristers AND solicitors can become judges.

## Suing a Solicitor or Barrister

It is possible to sue a solicitor for breach of contract as there is a contract between solicitor and client. However, there is **no such contract between a client and barrister.**

It is possible to sue a solicitor or a barrister for negligence in and out of court.

**Multiple Choice Questions - Section one – LO1 MCQs**

1. An example of a change in the Constitution is
   - a) The Abolition of the death Penalty 2001
   - b) Cigarette penalties 2004
   - c) Abolition of free plastic bags in shops 2003
   - d) Appointment of a new President

2. In 1972 an amendment to the Irish Constitution lowered the voting age to
   - a) 19
   - b) 21
   - c) 18
   - d) 16

3. What is the "burden of proof" that the prosecution has to establish for a jury to convict a defendant in Irish criminal cases?
   - a) on the balance of probabilities
   - b) depending on intention
   - c) beyond all doubt
   - d) beyond reasonable doubt

4. In which court will a case be brought against a defendant for speeding, TV licence or drink driving?
   - a) District Court
   - b) District Criminal Court
   - c) Circuit Civil Court
   - d) Circuit Criminal Court

5. What is the Statute of limitations for the tort of Negligence?
   - a) 1 year
   - b) 2 years
   - c) 3 years
   - d) 6 years

6. What is the Statute of limitations for the tort of Nuisance?
   - a) 1 year
   - b) 2 years
   - c) 3 years
   - d) 6 years

7. An example of Irish Secondary legislation is;
   - a) The Road Traffic Act
   - b) The Consumer Protection Act
   - c) Hiways and Byways Protection

d) Construction Regulations 2006–2012

8. Where does the European Commission have its offices?
   a) Dublin
   b) London
   c) Luxemburg
   d) Brussels

9. An example of EU Secondary legislation is;
   a) The Road Traffic Act
   b) The Consumer Protection Act
   c) Hiways and Byways Protection
   d) European Union (Batteries and Accumulators) Regulation.

10. Ireland joined the EU in?
    a) 1973
    b) 1959
    c) 1981
    d) 1990

11. The Supreme court in Ireland is the highest court in Ireland dealing with:
    a) National issues
    b) EU issues
    c) All issues
    d) Appeals cases only

12. A jury can be used in civil cases in Ireland where the case is a case on
    a) Negligence
    b) Nuisance
    c) Defamation
    d) Trespass

13. Which of the following is associated with private law?
    a) Constitution law
    b) Criminal law
    c) Civil law
    d) None of the above

14. Which of the following courts in the Irish legal system has criminal jurisdiction?
    a) District Civil Court
    b) Central Criminal Court
    c) Court of Civil Appeal
    d) Circuit Court

15.     Dan has been stopped for drunk driving, he is legally over the limit, and has been charged under the Road Traffic Act, he is fighting this case as he claims his car works on auto pilot and therefore the is not actually driving it, which statutory interpretation would the judge most likely use in this case to ensure that the law was adhered to?
a) Literal rule
b) Golden rule
c) Mischief rule
d) Ejudsum Generis rule

16.     Which of the following terms best describes the reason for the judge's decision?
a) Per incuriam
b) Obiter dicta
c) Ratio decidendi
d) None of the Above

17.     Which rule of interpretation involves an examination of the intention of the Oireachtas?
a) The golden rule
b) The literal rule
c) The mischief rule
d) The obiter rule

18.     Which of the following describes a statement that is made obiter dicta?
a) It is binding on all lower courts hearing similar cases
b) It is not binding unless made by the Supreme court
c) It is a statement made by the judge when summing up
d) None of the Above

19.     Those who come to equity must come with clean hands." – this is a _____.
a) Precedent
b) Maxim of equity
c) Obiter dictum
d) All of the above

20.     Which of the following is a maxim of equity
a) Those who seek equity must do impersoram
b) Those who come to equity may have dirty hands
c) Equity aids the vigilant not those who sleep on their rights
d) Those who come to equity must do so vigilantly

21.     Which of the following is NOT an equitable remedy
   a) Injunction
   b) Rescission
   c) Damages
   d) Mareva

22.     Which of the following is a common law remedy
   a) Specific performance
   b) Rectification
   c) Damages
   d) Injunction

23.     The modern Irish legal system came about when which systems combined
   a) Brehon laws and Common law
   b) Equity and Common law
   c) Brehon Law and Equity
   d) Civil law and common law

24.     The Oireachtas get its power to create legislation from;
   a) statute law
   b) precedent
   c) the constitution
   d) all of the above

25.     The two main divisions of law are
   a) Constitution law and statute
   b) Criminal law and statute
   c) Criminal law and civil law
   d) Civil law and Constitutional law

26.     The major differences between civil and criminal law is
   a) Civil law's burden of proof is less than criminal law
   b) Civil law has the same burden of proof as criminal law
   c) Criminal law's burden of proof is less than civil law
   d) Criminal law has no burden of proof, only standard of proof

27.     The role of the victim in a criminal trial is as;
   a) prosecution
   b) defendant
   c) witness
   d) none of the above

28.     A custodial sentence is a punishments for an offender who is guilty of;
   a) a criminal offence
   b) a breach of a consumer contract
   c) not getting required planning permission
   d) exceeding the agreed expenditure on sales contracts

29.     The Burden of Proof means
   a) The difficulties in proving the facts of the case
   b) The party who has to prove the facts of the case
   c) The amount of evidence the parties are required to have
   d) None of the above

30.     What is the standard of proof in civil law
   a) beyond reasonable doubt
   a) balance of probabilities
   b) what the judge believes
   c) what is fair just and reasonable

31.     The standard of proof in criminal law is
   a) balance of probabilities
   b) the best evidence presented
   c) beyond reasonable doubt
   d) what the legal teams produce to court

32.     The accused will be punished by
   a) A fine
   b) A custodial sentence
   c) Community service
   d) Probation

33.     The Oireachtas is made up of
   a) Courts, Dáil and President
   b) Dáil, Seanad and President
   c) Uachtaran na hEireann, Dáil and Courts
   d) Seanad and Dáil

34.     A Bill can only become law when it has passed by
   a) The Dáil
   b) The Seanad
   c) The Dáil and the Seanad
   d) The President

35.     When a Bill becomes a law it is called
   a) Act of the Oireachtas
   b) Statute
   c) Presidential Bill

d) a and b

36.     The literal rule means that the judge will interpret the Statue to mean
   a) what the legislature intended
   b) what the legal teams agreed to
   c) the ordinary meaning of the words used
   d) none of the above

37.     The golden rule means that the judge will interpret the Statue to mean
   a) what the legislature intended
   b) the interpretation of the words in the statute
   c) the argument put forward by counsel
   d) none of the above

38.     Under European Law a European Directive
   a) is implemented into national law by an act of the Oireachtas
   b) only needs implementation should Ireland wish to
   c) is directly effective from Europe as soon as it is past
   d) all of the above

39.     Under European Law a European Directive
   a) is implemented by an Act of the Oireachtas
   b) is directly binding on Ireland when it is passed in Europe
   c) is implemented on a stage basis by Ireland
   d) none of the above

40.     The decisions of courts outside of Ireland are
   a) binding
   b) original
   c) persuasive
   d) dissenting

41.     The courts of first instance in Ireland are
   a) District Court and Supreme Court
   b) Circuit Court and High Court
   c) Central Criminal Court and the Court of Appeal
   d) The Special Criminal Court and the Supreme Court

42.     The highest Court in Ireland is
   a) Court of Appeal
   b) Circuit Court
   c) Supreme Court
   d) The District Court

43.    You have been arrested on a summary offence. This means that
   a) the case will be heard by a judge sitting alone
   b) the case will be heard by a judge and jury
   c) the maximum sentence is 12 months
   d) the sentenced will be a minimum of 24 months
      1. A only
      2. A and c
      3. C only

44.    The accused solicitor has told them that their offence is an indictable offence tried summarily, this means:
   a) it is a serious offence tried in the District Court before a judge and jury
   b) it is a minor offence tried in the Circuit Court with a judge sitting alone with no jury
   c) it is an offence which is indictable in nature, but with the client and prosecution's consent it can be heard by the District Court judge
   d) it is an offence which is summary in nature, and with the defence's consent it can be heard by the District Court judge

45.    Where a court applies a precedent from another Jurisdiction, this precedent is said to be
   a) Binding
   b) Authorative
   c) Persuasive
   d) Permissible

46.    A statutory instrument is
   a) Primary legislation
   b) Secondary/delegated legislation
   c) Common law legislation
   d) Precedent

47.    A European Directive
   a) Is implemented into Nation law by an Act of the Oireachtas
   b) Has no requirement to be enacted into Irish law by the Oireachtas
   c) Has direct effect into Irish law as soon as it is passed in Europe
   d) All of the above

48.    The Courts of First Instance in Ireland are
   a) Where the legal proceedings are finalised

    b) Where the legal proceedings are initiated
    c) Where the parties can appeal a decision
    d) None of the above

49.    Where the accused is sentenced in the District Court and they appeal their case, if they lose this case, their maximum sentence will be
    a) 6 months
    b) 12 months
    c) 24 months
    d) 9 months

50.    Where the damages in a personal injury case are estimated at €60,500, the case will be heard in the;
    a) Circuit Criminal Court
    b) District Court
    c) Circuit Civil Court
    d) High Court

## Section 2 – LO2 - TORT

### Types of Tort

**Intentional torts**; such as trespass, nuisance, false imprisonment, passing off, defamation,
**Unintentional torts,** such as negligence,
**Strict liability** (*no requirement to prove fault, once the damage was done the plaintiff has a case*) torts such as manufacturer's product liability.

### Aims of Tort

**Compensation** - to compensate the victim of the wrong to the extent of the damage suffered!
**Deterrence / prevention** - to ensure that it does not happen again or, even, better, to prevent it from occurring at all

### How does a tort differ from a crime?

A tort will lead the wronged party to try and recover money as compensation for the loss or injury suffered. A tort does not, however, call upon the state to punish the wrongdoer.

### Negligence

Is as a result of conduct that falls below the standard of care which is demanded for the protection of others against the unreasonable risk of harm. The test in negligence;

- the plaintiff (persons suffering from the harm) must show that the defendant (person causing the harm) owed them a duty of care; and.
- they breached that duty of care, (by falling below the standard of care); and;
- their breach caused the other person injuries; and;
- caused them to suffer reasonably foreseeable harm (damage was not too remote).

## Duty of care

This is the duty owed by one person to another, we must prove that there is a duty (*a requirement to take care*), or it can be automatic as in parent child, employer employee, **Donoghue v Stevenson** = you must take care that your actions do not affect your neighbour, (*proximity and foreseeability*) **Caparo Industries v. Dickman Plc** = same as above 1) proximity and 2) foreseeability PLUS also 3) fair, just and reasonable.

**Professional duty of care**, this is where a professional in their job is held to have a higher standard than a layperson, therefore higher standard of professional duty of care, i.e. a doctors stops at an accident and the patent dies, good Samaritan laws protect an ordinary citizen who stops to try and help, whereas a doctor merely driving by "off duty" will still be help to the professional standard of care.

## Breach (standard)

If you do owe a duty and hurt your neighbour the court will see if you acted like a reasonable person would, would a person with your skills and qualifications and experience had done that, (*reach above or fall below that standard*),

## Causation

This means did your behaviour cause the damage to the other person; (*did your actions fall below the standard of a reasonable person who owed you a duty to take care?*)

## Remoteness

If you did owe a duty and you did breach that duty and your actions fell below those of a reasonable person, was that damage cause reasonably foreseeable ( *would you have ever thought that could have happened, i.e. I never thought in a million years that would happen*)

## Strict liability

Product/manufacturer liability. **Manufacturers Strict Liability**

Negligence-based product liability is based on a manufacturer's breach of the reasonable standard of care and failing to make a product safe. This is a no fault principle, fault does not need to be proved, and that fact that the item was faulty and caused damage is sufficient. *In other words, even if a person did not actually do something that caused injury, something they own, did.*

## Statute of limitations

**(TORT)** 6 years for trespass, nuisance etc.,
*HOWEVER*, **Personal Injury** is two years
**Defamation** = one year – statute of limitations act 1957.

## Misrepresentation

a) innocent misrepresentation
Representative makes a statement which he reasonably believes to be true

b) negligent misrepresentation
Representative makes a statement which he believes is true but has no reasonable grounds

c) fraudulent misrepresentation, fraud
Representative makes a statement which they do not honestly believe in his statement (KNOWS IT IS NOT TRUE!)

## Trespass to Person

**Assault** occurs when one person deliberately leads a person to believe they are about to be harmed. Direct act causing fear (includes silent phone calls)
Elements of assault are:
- Mental state of the defendant
- The effect on plaintiff
- Capability to carry out the threat
- Words

**Battery** occurs when one person unlawfully touches another person. It is intentional and direct application of force (bringing an actual item in contact with the body of another person)
Elements of battery are:
- The mental state of the defendant
- The defendant's act was under his control
- Contact
- Without plaintiff's consent/permission

**False Imprisonment** – to restrict a person's movement *(arresting, imprisoning or preventing person from leaving)*
Elements in False Imprisonment are:

- Intention is essential
- The restraint must be a direct result of the defendant's act
- The restraint must be complete

## Defences to tort of trespass

a) Consent (agreed to it)
b) Self-defence (had to protect themselves)
c) Defence of third parties (had to do it to protect another person)
d) Lawful arrest (citizen's arrest, only when they believe they have, or are about to, commit an criminal offence)
e) Defence of property (stop someone from damaging their property)
f) Duress (under pressure, threatened if they did not commit the tort)

## Trespass to Goods – Conversion

Taking someone's property and using it for their own personal gain. Dealing with the personal goods of another person denying the right of the owner to the goods. Only the owner of the goods can bring a claim for conversion.
**For Example**: *For example, if a farmer has 9 large trees growing on their property, another neighbour cuts them down, the neighbour may be liable for conversion, even if they don't use the trees, they denied the owner use of the trees even if it was only for shade or producing fruit.*

## Sample conversion

- Contradicting the title of the true owner
- Detaining goods belonging to the owner without permission after a demand for the goods which has been refused.
- Destruction of goods belonging to the owner
- Selling goods without the owner's permission.

## Trespass to Goods – Detinue

Wrongful failure/refusal to return goods when demand has been made for same.
The plaintiff must be in possession or have an immediate claim for possession.

Reasonable period of time for return is allowed.  Each case is taken on its own merit, i.e. reasonable time for fast moving consumer goods will not be the same as for furniture, and the reasonable time is relative to the case.

The tests for detinue are:
- Possession
- Demand made
- Demand receive
- Refusal or failure to return
- No excuse of necessity, authority

## Trespass to Land

Trespass to land, the form of trespass most associated with the term 'trespass' refers to the "wrongful interference with one's possessory rights in [real] property.
The Irish constitution states that we have the right to private property without intrusion.
For example: *Hill-walkers must understand that trespassing on private farmland is an intrusion (disturbance), an intrusion on farmers' rights and livelihoods (earning a living).  For instance hill walkers going through fields and leaving gates open not only disturb farmers, but could allow livestock to escape and cause damage or be killed or even that other animals could get onto the land and cause damage.*

Trespass to land involves one or a combination of the following acts without lawful justification:
1. Entering land that is owned by the plaintiff.
2. Remaining on the land.
3. Placing objects or projections onto the land

Elements of trespass to land are:
- a) Intention
- b) Acts of entry done voluntary
- c) Interference is foreseeable as due to defendant's act
- d) Interference must be direct

## Private Nuisance

A private nuisance is a continuous, unlawful and indirect interference with the use or enjoyment of land, or of some right over or in connection with it. Cases of private nuisance often involve neighbours and are caused by noise, smell, vibrations, animals, trees and incursions by other such items.

Judging liability is a **balancing act**: occupiers are entitled to 'reasonable comfort' but no more.

The following factors must be considered in a nuisance action:

1. Locus Standi; (legal right to bring the case)
2. Conduct - acts or omissions; (are the act or omissions (not acting) causing the nuisance)
3. Damage or Interference; (is there actual damage or interference with the right to enjoyment)
4. Strict liability for Material Damage;
5. Liability for interference with enjoyment judged by standard of unreasonable impact.

## Defences to Private Nuisance

### Consent

Where the claimant by their actions, consent to the nuisance, i.e. *Thomas v Lewis*: The defendant opened quarry & granted grazing rights to the claimant. **HELD:** When the claimant acceptance the grazing rights the consented to the acquiescence to the nuisance.

### Prescription

If the nuisance has been continued for 20 years without interruption the defendant will not liable if s/he pleads a prescriptive right to the nuisance.

### Statutory Authority

There will be a defence to private nuisance if it can be shown that the activities complained of by the claimant were authorised (expressly or impliedly) by a statute.

### Coming to the nuisance is no defence.

The claimant moving to the area where the nuisance is occurring is no defence. See above *Bliss v Hall*

## Public Nuisance

A nuisance can become a public nuisance whether the effects on the public are from its source, its destination or the final effect. All public nuisance cases are looked at from the point of "reasonableness".

Examples of public nuisance include, *obstruction of public roads, obstruction of access to business access to workplaces, noises pollution, the enjoyment of paths, roads, parks, forests, it water supply contamination, oil spillage from the activities of large oil companies and this includes but is not limited to carrying on abhorrent business like operating a brothel.*

## Defences in nuisance

### Consent

Where the claimant by their actions consent to the nuisance

### Prescription

If the nuisance has been continued for 20 years without interruption

### Statutory Authority

There will be a defence to private nuisance if it can be shown that the activities complained of by the claimant were authorised (expressly or impliedly) by a statute.

### Coming to the nuisance is no defence.

The claimant moving to the area where the nuisance is no defence.

## Remedies for Nuisance

## Damages

### Compensation –

The compensation will depend on the amount of damage done, i.e. interference with enjoyment will be amenity value (the value you placed on aesthetics, visual or quality of life)

### Injunctions

Injunctions are equitable remedies given at the discretion of the court (*see law of equity in my Introduction to the Irish Legal System book*).  They are **Mandatory** (*make you do something*) or **Prohibitory** (*stop you from doing something*).  The difference between a mandatory and prohibitory: (*i.e. The council can get a mandatory injunction to make you clean your yard, whereas they cannot get a prohibitory injunction to stop you not cleaning your yard..!! And vice versa, the council can get a prohibitory injunction to stop you having farm animals at your urban house, whereas they cannot get a mandatory injunction to make you not have them...*)Due to the on-going nature of the tort, injunctions are often sought. This is an equitable remedy, and therefore a discretionary remedy, and may or may not be awarded in addition to damages.

***Interim,*** these are emergency orders which are ordered to stop some act or omission immediately, there will then be an application for a:

***Permanent injunction****:* an injunction which remains in force perpetually (*forever).*

## Abatement

This is the remedy of self-help, e.g. removing over-hanging tree branches, which are a nuisance. (Make sure to return the branches to the owner)

## Remedies for public nuisance

### Damages

An award for damages can be sought by the plaintiff, however, these are minimal, they serve not to punish the wrong doer, but to encourage the defendant to take steps to negate or stop the nuisance.

### Injunctions

Due to the on-going nature of the tort, injunctions are often sought. This is an equitable remedy, and therefore a discretionary remedy, and may or may not be awarded in addition to damages.

***Interim,*** these are emergency orders which are ordered to stop some act or omission immediately, there will then be an application for a:

***Permanent injunction****;* this is an injunction which remains in force perpetually.

Injunctions can consist of a;

***Mandatory injunction****,* an order to compel the defendant to carry out a particular act, i.e. clear a pathway or roadway or a;

***Prohibitory injunction,*** this injunction is ordered by the court to stop the defendant for committing an act, which occasionally can include noise abatement orders.

## Strict Liability

Theory of strict liability started with **_Rylands v. Fletcher_**
Defendant's liability for strict liability is without regard to: _Fault, Foreseeability, Standard of Care or Causation._ **Liability is based on dangerous activities**.
It is a liability that exists even though the defendant was not negligent.

- Engaging in dangerous activities—storing flammable liquids.
- Owning animals—having a dog bite someone
- Sale of goods that are dangerous

In other words, even if <u>a person</u> did not actually do something that caused injury, something they own, did.

## Manufacturers Strict Liability

Negligence-based product liability is based on a manufacturer's breach of the reasonable standard of care and failing to make a product safe. This tort is liability without fault based on public policy:
Consumers are protected from unsafe products;
- Manufacturers should be liable to any user of the product;
- Manufacturers, sellers and distributors can bear the costs of injuries.

Manufacturer must exercise "due care" in:
- Designing products;
- Manufacturing and Assembling Products;
- Inspecting and Testing Products; and
- Placing adequate warning labels

## Vicarious Liability

The liability of one person (principal/employer) for actions of another person (agent/employee), who was acting on principal's behalf.
In negligence cases, most often involves employers and employees or principals and agents. The employer is responsible for torts committed by employees while at work and ACTING on the employers instructions

# Defamation

**Defamation** is an untrue statement about a person which lowers their reputation in the eyes of the general public. Defamation is the wrongful act of <u>injuring</u> another's <u>reputation</u> by <u>making false statements</u>.
- slander—spoken defamation
- libel- written or printed defamation

However in Ireland, libel and slander are classed as just one tort of defamation.

## To be defamatory the statement must be:
- <u>False</u>
- <u>Communicated to a 3rd party</u>
- <u>The victim's reputation is ruined or he/she faces ridicule</u>

<u>The case must be taken within one year (two with special court permissions)</u>

> **Quigley V Creation** = if a certain amount of the community hold a negative view of the plaintiff due to the defamation of the defendant there is cause for action (able to sue)
>
> **Speight V Gosnay** = the original publisher is liable for republished materials even if they were not aware of the publication.

## Defences to Defamation.

Truth is normally an absolute defence.
Statement was privileged:
Absolute: judicial and legislative (Dáil/parliament) proceedings.
Qualified: good faith, limited.
Public Figures: plaintiff must show statement made with "actual malice."

## Case Law (Tort "general")

> **McKenna Vs. Best Travel;** = Plaintiff was injured when there was civil unrest in Bethlehem, there was a stone thrown at her through the window of the bus, although the Defendant owed her a duty of care, the court ruled that defendant was <u>not liable as they had no specialised knowledge of the risk.</u>
>
> **Re Polemis** = There was no requirement that the damage was foreseeable. The defendant was liable for all the direct consequences of their action, i.e. the specific harm (injury) did not have to be foreseeable, only the requirement of foreseeing any harm is required.

**Moynihan V Moynihan** = grandmother was liable for the actions of the aunt when the grandchild was scaled as she was acting on the grandmothers instructions

**Grant V the Australian Knitting Mills** = Negligence, **neighbour** principle applies, and defendant is held liable for extra sulphites in the manufacturing.

## Defence in Tort

1. **Inevitable accident**
   no reasonable precaution would have prevented the occurrence of the accident. The circumstances of the incident will determine reasonableness
   *Stanley V Powell (1891)*
2. **Consent of plaintiff**
   *Volentif non fit injura* – to the willing there can be no injury. Where a person is aware of all of the material facts and yet comes to the injury cannot claim afterwards for physical risks. *Regan V Irish Automobile Club (1990)*
3. **Contributory Negligence**
   Where the Plaintiff contributes to their own injuries, they may not receive the full compensation in their action.
4. **Illegality**
   This maxim states that; from an evil cause no action arises. *Anderson V Cooke 2005*

**Remedies** = how to fix it, there is common law and equitable remedies in tort, such as (equitable) injunctions, and damages are common law.

## Damages

**Nominal** - defendant has committed a tort, but the claimant has suffered no loss. **Contemptuous**, means you win, but you shouldn't have brought this case, award could be 1 cent.
**Special** = can be calculated, i.e. wages, doctors, etc.
**General** = cannot be calculated, such as pain and suffering.
**Aggravated** = actions which further shock the plaintiff, and
**Exemplary** = shocked the court.

## Injunctions

- mandatory injunction (make defendant do something)
- prohibitory injunction (stop the defendant doing something)
- interim (temporary)

- interlocutory (an order while awaiting the outcome of an interim order)
- perpetual (a permanent injunction)

## Losses

### Pecuniary losses:

(quantifiable) Ascertainable or possibly agreed amounts of money

### Non pecuniary losses

(unknown amounts of money) will have to be defined by court.

### Liquidated damages

Damages which are agreed before the contract is formed, i.e. a set amount that will be paid if the contract is breached or the terms not adhered to.

### Unliquidated damages

Amounts of money which cannot be foreseen or assessed, the judge will assed and decide.

## Elements of Passing off

Traders are forbidden from selling their goods in such as a way as to entice customers to buy their goods by deceiving them into believing they are those of a competitor.

**The test:** the three fundamental elements of passing off are Reputation, Misrepresentation and Damage to goodwill. These three elements are also known as the *Classical Trinity*, as restated by the House of Lords in the case of *Reckitt & Colman Ltd V Borden INC* . It was stated in this case that in a suit for passing off the plaintiff must establish:

1. Goodwill or reputation attached to his goods or services.
2. They must prove a misrepresentation by the defendant to the public i.e. leading or likely to lead the public to believe that the goods and services offered by him are that of the plaintiff's.
3. They must demonstrate that he has suffered a loss due to the belief that the defendant's goods and services are those of the plaintiff's.

## Multiple Choice Questions - Section Two - LO 2 MCQs

1.  What is the standard of care applied to professionals with a special skill or expertise?
    a)  That of the reasonable person with the same skill or expertise
    b)  That of the reasonable person in that profession
    c)  That of the reasonably qualified person
    d)  That of the reasonable person with the same level of experience or skill in that profession.

2.  What does a claimant need to show to establish liability in a negligence claim?
    1.  There was a duty of care
    2.  That the duty was not breached
    3.  The breach caused damage
    4.  The damage was foreseeable
    a)  1, 2 and 4 only
    b)  1, 3 and 4 only
    c)  2 and 3 only
    d)  All of the above

3.  What does the *"eggshell skull"* rule mean?
    a)  That defendant is not liable where the plaintiff had a pre-existing injury
    b)  That defendants must take their victims as they find them
    c)  The defendant is liable for injuries which would be foreseen by a reasonable person
    d)  None of the above

4.  Which of the following may give rise to vicarious liability?
    1.  Vehicle owners and their permitted drivers.
    2.  Employer and employee.
    3.  Teachers and pupils in their care during school hours.
    a)  1 and 2 only
    b)  1 and 3 only
    c)  2 and 3 only
    d)  1, 2 and 3 only

5.  Which case ruled that where a person who is visiting the house, acts on the instruction of the owner of the property, the owner is liable for their acts?
    a)  Re Polomis
    b)  Hadley v Baxendale
    c)  Speight V Gosnay
    d)  Moynihan v Moynihan

6. Define the meaning of the defence *volenti non fit injuria*?
   a) There is no liability on the defendant where the plaintiff has voluntary assumed the risk
   b) The person who causes the injury must be held liable
   c) The compensation must fit the damages
   d) None of the above

7. Where a defendant can prove contributory negligence against the plaintiff, they are proving
   a) The plaintiff did not contribute to their own injuries
   b) The defendant contributed to the plaintiffs injuries
   c) The plaintiff contributed to their own injuries
   d) None of the above

8. Sarah is learning to drive; she is negligent and mounts the kerb, injuring her driving instructor, what is Sarah's duty of care in this case
   a) There is a driver to driver duty of care owed
   b) The duty owed is that of a reasonable learner driver
   c) The duty of care is that owed by a learner driver
   d) All of the Above

9. Interference with another's enjoyment of life or property is known as:
   a) Trespass
   b) Nuisance
   c) Defamation
   d) None of the above

10. A wrongful act that injures another's reputation with false statements is known as:
    a) Trespass
    b) Nuisance
    c) Defamation
    d) None of the above

11. The failure to exercise the degree of care that a reasonable person would exercise those results in the proximate cause of actual harm to an innocent person is known as:
    a) Strict Liability
    b) Nuisance
    c) Defamation
    d) Negligence

12. The tort that results when one person deliberately frightens another person into the reasonable belief that he or she is about to be injured is known as:
    a) Assault
    b) Battery
    c) Assault and Battery
    d) Grievous bodily harm

13. Manufacturers product Strict Liability requires
    a) Fault
    b) No fault
    c) Damage
    d) None of the above

14. The rule in **_Mc Kenna V Best travel_** stated that
    a) There were liable as they had brought the defendant to a dangerous territory
    b) They were not liable as they had got the plaintiff to sign a disclaimer before leaving
    c) There were not guilty as they had no specialised knowledge of the risks
    d) They were not guilty as the plaintiff had voluntarily went to the danger

15. The requirement that, the damage need not be foreseeable was a ruling in the case of:
    a) Hadley v Baxendale
    b) Carlill v Carbolic smokeball
    c) Re Polomis
    d) Quigley v Creation

16. The court ruling in **_Speight v Gosnay_** stated that:
    a) Where a statement lowers the applicant in the eyes of a community the defendant is liable in defamation
    b) The applicant can bring a case in defamation if they receive a defamatory letter from an individual; they are the only ones to read it.
    c) The defendant is liable if the plaintiff reads the defamatory statement and is upset
    d) The defendant is liable if another person republishes the defamatory statement even if it is withdrawn by the original poster

17. Liquidated damages are
    a) Quantifiable
    b) Unquantifiable
    c) Unknown

d) None of the above

18. ***Grant v Australian Knitting Mills*** involved
   a) Negligence
   b) Nuisance
   c) Defamation
   d) Assault

19. The Irish precedent case in defining the Duty of Care owed is:
   a) Donoghue v Stevenson
   b) Carlill v Carbolic Smokeball
   c) Glencar v Mayo Co Co
   d) Caparo Industries v Dickman Plc.

20. Remoteness of damages can be defined as:
   a) Proximity of the parties
   b) Duty of care owed
   c) Reasonable Foreseeability
   d) Standard of Care

21. Which of the following is a defence in Nuisance
   a) It is a quarry, there will be noise
   b) The levels of noise are acceptable
   c) Prescription
   d) All of the above

22. Strict liability occurs when;
   a) There is no requirement to find fault
   b) Fault must be established
   c) Fault is established one the duty of care is established
   d) The parties agree there is fault

23. The tort of passing off occurs when
   a) A seller sells his own goods on his own market stalls
   b) A seller sells goods and leads buyers to believe they are the goods of a competitor
   c) A buyer believes the goods on sale are branded goods and buys them
   d) A seller tells the buyer the goods look like those of a competitor but they are not

24. Interference with another's enjoyment of life or property is known as
   a) Defamation
   a) Tort
   b) Trespass to the Person
   c) Nuisance

25. The tort of Conversion is defined as;
    a) a person lending a neighbor their lawnmower
    b) taking another person property and using for personal gain
    c) giving property back to the owner when they ask for it
    d) none of the above

26. The tort that results when one person deliberately frightens another person into the reasonable belief that he or she is about to be injured is known as:
    a) conversion
    b) tort
    c) assault
    d) battery

27. Failure to return goods to the owner when requested is called;
    a) conversion
    b) nuisance
    c) trespass to the person
    d) detinue

28. Prescription is a defence to
    a) nuisance
    b) trespass to land
    c) nuisance
    d) defamation

29. Statutory Authority gets its power from
    a) legislation
    b) common law
    c) prescription
    d) case law

30. **_Res Ipsa Loquitur_** means.
    a) the solicitor speaks with the prosecution
    b) the thing speaks for itself
    c) the defendant speaks for themself
    d) the barrister speaks for the defendant

31. Liability for dangerous or "unnatural things" stems from the case of;
    a) Donoghue v Stevenson
    b) Hadley v Baxendale
    c) Quigley v Creation
    d) Rylands v Fletcher

32. Despite the defendant not having done anything wrong, they may still be held liable in tort under:

a) negligence
b) strict liability
c) defamation
d) trespass

33. An employer's liability for the actions of their employee, who is acting outside the scope of their employment, or outside their working time, has;
a) vicarious liability
b) no liability
c) employers liability
d) employees' rights at work

34. Slander is defined as;
a) the spoken word
b) the written word
c) words found online
d) none of the above

35. Libel is defined as;
a) the spoken word
b) the written word
c) words found online
d) none of the above

36. In defamation, opinions are generally
a) actionable
b) non actionable
c) libellous
d) slanderous

37. In defamation, republication is actionanable as per;
a) Quigley v Creation
b) Speight v Gosney
c) Donoghue v Stevenson
d) Hadley v Baxendale

38. To be defamatory, a statement must,
a) be told to the defendant
b) be told to the general public
c) be communicated to a third party
d) be thought by the defendant

39. Which case laid down the precedent in determining the duty of care?
a) Donoghue v Stevenson
b) Fischer v bell

c) Caparo Industries v Dickman Plc.
d) Partridge v Crittenden

40. Mitigation of losses means;
a) The defendant must take reasonable care to ensure they do not damage the plaintiff's goods
b) The plaintiff must take reasonable steps to reduce their own losses
c) The plaintiff must take every step possible to reduce their own losses
d) The defendant must take reasonable steps to reduce their plaintiff's losses

41. Which of the following cases resulted in the court finding that cost of avoiding the risk outweighed the risk and found that the defendant was not negligent
a) The Wagon Mound 2
b) Latimer v AEC
c) Donoghue v Stevenson
d) Caparo Industries v Dickman Plc.

42. The case of **McGhee v National Coal Board** is relevant to
a) The "but for" test
b) Causation
c) Remoteness of damage
d) Material contribution test

43. Which of the following is NOT a type of damages
a) Nominal damages
b) Exemplary damages
c) Aggravated damages
d) Contemporary damages

44. Which case was the claimant found to have contributed to their injuries
a) Livox Quarries v Boyce
b) Jones v Boyce
c) Jones v Livox Quarries
d) Smith v Jones

45. Contributory negligence occurs when:
a) The claimant was hurt because of the actions of the defendant
b) The claimant was a reasonable person who was hurt due to another's actions
c) The claimant was wholly or partly to blame for their own injuries
d) The claimant was an innocent victim in an accident

46. How does the courts best determine if an employer is vicariously liable for the actions of staff?
    a) Control test
    b) The reasonable man test
    c) Proximity test
    d) Fair just and reasonable

47. What is the closest description of the *reasonable man*
    a) He is very cautious
    b) He is very safety conscious
    c) He was low intelligence
    d) He is neither very cautious nor does he take excessive risks

48. Which of the following is least likely to win a case for breach of duty of care
    a) A doctor giving the wrong medication
    b) A garda not taking a dangerous criminals fingerprint
    c) A dentist giving the wrong anaesthetic
    d) A solicitor is careless in conducting his client's case

49. What is the purpose of determining if a duty of care exists
    a) To ensure that all parties are treated fairly
    b) To determine who is liable for the damage
    c) It ensure that the right person is sued
    d) To determine if the wrongdoer was actually careless

50. Why did Mrs. Donoghue bring an action in tort and not in contract?
    a) She was not a party to the contract and therefore the only avenue was tort
    b) She had a contract which was frustrated so had to bring an action in tort
    c) She had the ginger beer drank before she seen the snail so contract was discharged
    d) She bought the ginger beer with her friends money so she had no contract

## Section 3 – LO3 - CONTRACT

### Offer and acceptance

**Offer** is a clear, concise statement which, when made was intended to be binding, which is distinguished from an invitation to treat which is an offer by the seller for the buyer to make them an offer.

### Invitation to treat

An invitation by the seller for the buyer to make THEM an offer.

**Acceptance** is where there is acceptance of the terms of the offer.

### Privity of contract

Generally speaking, only those a party to the contract can claim in any action. However, there are certain exceptions, for instance, *the rights of children under a parents health insurance,* the right of third parties, say for instance a third parties right to sue another drivers insurance and receive pay-out even though they are not involved in the contract. Etc.

**Consideration**
Quid pro quo, something for something, something of value.

**Part payment of debt**
Part payment is not good consideration under the **Pinnel case,** however in modern time *promissory estoppel* can be used if a party takes the promise to forego the rest of the debt and acts on it. (if the bank agrees to take less and you pay this amount for some time the bank cannot come back in a year and look for more, as the party relied on this agreement.)

**Innominate terms**
These are terms which a person may not believe are either a condition or a warranty. If the situation is that one party believes it is a condition and the other a warranty the judge will have to decide. (example) if you buy a car from a garage and one week later the engine blows up, you as a buyer may believe this is a condition (car cannot drive without an engine) and the garage owner may believe it is a warranty (will run when its fixed), as you cannot agree as both parties have a point, the courts will determine which one it is.

### Expressed term

This is something which has either been stated or agreed to either in writing or verbally

### Implied term

This is something that is assumed or it is taken as not needed to be spoken, for instance, if you buy a kettle it is implied it will boil water, however, you will not see this written on the box.

### Exemption clause

This is a clause which one party can put into the contract before the contract starts so that their liability is reduced or excluded should something go wrong, however these clauses must be incorporated" inserted" legally, and can be by signature, agreement, past use or notice.

### Specific Performance

This is an equitable remedy (*at the discretion of the court, means you cannot get it as of right but can apply for it*), it means the defendant must perform the tasks as specified in the contract, such as a plumber who comes in and only partially does the job and leaves, however it cannot be used for employment "employee" contracts or one to one contracts, (*self-employed "plumber, electrician accountant etc." in not an employee*), it cannot be used to make someone pay upfront, it cannot be given where the court cant oversee it, it cannot be given to minors or where it is unjust or unfair (*i.e. if the plumber was in the middle of your job and had an accident and now wheelchair bound and unable to work, the courts would not grant an order for specific performance*)

### Damages

**Special** (the damage can be exactly measured in money, i.e. wages and medical bills).
**General** (*they cannot be assessed exactly, i.e. pain and suffering*)
**Aggravated** (*these are damages that result from the defendants behaviour, such as mental distress, pain, anguish, grief, anxiety*)
**Punitive** (to deter future bad behaviour, malicious, oppressive etc.)
**Nominal** (this is where no actual harm is done but a right is violated "*such as right of way being refused etc.*")

## Discharge of Debt

This relieves a borrower from his or her obligations to a lender by a legal order of the court. For instance debts are discharged when a person becomes bankrupt, the debt is discharged, after one year they are a discharged bankrupt, or they can settle their debts and be discharged by the creditors.(if under one year)

## Evidentiary requirements in contracts

In Ireland, parties to a contract who wish to bring certain contract cases before the courts must have their contracts evident in writing, the rules pertaining to this rule stem from old contracts, where the courts otherwise may have to deem who is "the best liar", in order to combat the likelihood of fraud the Statute of Frauds (Ireland) Act 1695 was enacted, Section 2,specifically applies to four main types of contract:
1. Contracts to pay the debt of another.
2. Contracts where the consideration is to be married.
3. Contracts for the sale of land or an interest therein.
4. Contracts that will not be performed within one year.

## Tenders

**White v. Bluett** = No consideration, not complaining was not valid consideration

**Harvela Investments Ltd. V Royal trust Co. of Canada** = referential bids are not valid, as a contract needs a price, not a bid over the highest one

## Case law

**Felthouse V Bindley** = silence is not acceptance, nephew did not tell the uncle he was buying the horse.

**Edwards V Skyways** = commercial contact is implied to be binding. Pilot agreed to stop contributing to pension scheme I return for payment, he stopped the airline didn't pay, saying no intention was there.

**Stilk V Myrick** = some crew deserted a ship, the captain said would give the deserters wages to the remaining staff, held... no new consideration was given for the extra money and therefore no consideration, the staff were not entitled to promised wages.

**Hartley V Ponsonby** = The crew were entitled to the extra payment promised on the grounds that either they had gone beyond their existing contractual duty or that the voyage had become too dangerous frustrating the original contract and leaving the crew free to negotiate a new contract.

**Glasbrook Bros V Glamorgan County Council** = providing extra police in case of riot, In providing additional police to that required, the police had gone beyond their existing duty. They were therefore entitled to payment.

**Revenue Commissioners V Moroney** = promissory estoppel, family agreement which was never intended to be binding, revenue tried to make the family transfer land, court held no intention and estoppel allowed. May only be used as defence – 'as a shield, not as a sword'.

**Lowry V Reid** = Specific Performance, promise to give land to one son if he signed hi land to another son, later revoked in will,

## *Implied contracts*

Unwritten contracts implied is where it does not need to be said.

## *Expressed contracts*

Written or oral contracts where the terms of the contract are expressed by both parties.

## *Voidable contracts*

Duress, undue influence,
**Contracting signing AFTER agreement**
    **Spurling V Bradshaw** = contract signed after the contract agreed, however they had previous dealings so no right to sue.

## *Misrepresentation*

A false statement of fact made by one party to another party, which has the effect of inducing that party into the contract. Negligent, fraudulent and innocent.

**Innocent,** (believed what they were saying was true)
**Negligent** (careless as to whether it was true or not)
**Fraudulent** (knew what they were saying was a lie)

## *Mistake*

**Common mistake** - Where both parties make the same mistake
**Mutual mistake** - Where the parties are at cross purposes
**Unilateral mistake** - Where only one party is mistaken

### Illegality

Any contract which is illegal is not enforceable.

*Duress and undue influence*

**Duress,** when a contract is made using threat of violence,
**Undue influence,** when a person tries to take advantage of a position of power over another person or party

## Capacity

Mental capacity to enter contact = age, mental illness, drunkenness

### Part Performance of a Contract

**Cutter V Powell –Performance**–not finishing a contract because he died, the contract stated start to finish, he didn't finish. In modern legal systems the maxim of quantum meruit would come into play.

## Unconsciousable Bargain

This means that the contract is grossly unfair on one party, it occurs when one part does not receive a fair or just part in a contract, such as happened in the case of the farmer in **Grealish v Murphy.** The elderly Grealish, a farmer, lived alone in a rural part of Ireland, he was wealthy but only because of his property, the defendant agreed with Grealish to take care of him in return for signing the property on his death to him. Grealish got legal advice but it was not enough, he was under a false impression of his rights.

### Defences to unconciousable bargain
The onus of proof is on defendant. They must show that
1. independent legal advice was taken
2. the property was sold for market value
3. the plaintiff was aware of what was going on

## Discharging a contract, including discharge by frustration and exceptions to discharge by frustration

### *Frustration rules,*

1) unforeseeable, (by a reasonable person)
2) cause a radical change, (the contract is now very different to that agreed)
3) change in the obligations, (one party may have all the obligations or more, or less, than original agreed)
4) not caused by either party(neither party contributed to the incident)

## Contract Add-ons (addendums)

A contract can have additions added to them as long as both parties are aware of the changes and sign to accept them

## Hadley V Baxendate

Compensation is limited to the amount which arises directly from the breach or could reasonably be contemplated.

## Law of Agency

## Ratification

This happens when the principle is not immediately aware of the contract which the agent has entered on their behalf, however the minute they become aware of it and agrees to it (or say nothing even when they become aware) then the contract is ratified from the agent to the principle.

## Agency by estoppel

An *agency by estoppel* is created when a principal doesn't stop an agent from going beyond the agent's normal duties, which then gives the impression that an agency relationship has been established.

Say you're the owner of a car (**principle**) and you tell your friend (**agent**) to show the car (*normal duties*) to a possible buyer (**third party**). You inform the buyer that you will not be able to attend the time agreed but you were sending your friend on your behalf. Your friend shows the buyer the car, however your friend negotiates agree a price, even though you didn't give your friend any direct authority to do so. The buyer agrees to the agent's terms, goes and gets a loan to buy the car, then you say you will not sell the car for that price, and that you had not given your friend the power to sell it, merely show it to the buyer, the buyer can ESTOP you from going back on the agent agreement, because the buyer assumes the agent has the authority to act, therefore creating a contract, and an agency by estoppel has been created.

## Ostensible/Apparent Authority

Apparent authority refers to a situation where a reasonable third party would understand that an agent had authority to act. The situation above, the buyer would have a reasonable belief that your friend had the power to sell the car as:

1) he was acting on your behalf and;
2) you never said they didn't have any power or authority.

### *Actual Authority:*

You the (**Principal**) instruct your friend the (**Agent**) to sell the car to the buy the (**third party**) on your behalf.

**Express Authority: Oral or written instructions create the authority**

***Implied Authority:* Principal's conduct or trade customs create authority. Example; a car showroom selling cars.**

### Contracting inside/outside authority

If an agent is acting inside authority they are given (they are going by the instructions of the principle) they will not be liable for any losses, (to the principle or third party). If the agent is acting outside the authority given (they are ignoring the instructions of the principle) to them they will be liable to pay back the (principle only, principle must still pay the 3rd party, the third party can never lose out)

### Agency by Ratification

Where the agent takes it upon themselves to act on the principles behalf, when the principle becomes aware of it they agree to the terms, to ratify something is to change it. The rules in relation to ratification, 1) the principle must have existed 2)principle must have all of the facts, 3) it must be done in a reasonable time.

### Agency by necessity /emergency

Where an emergency occurs and the agent acts on the principles behalf without the principles knowledge, the rules for emergency agency are,
1) there must be a genuine emergency,
2) you must have tried to contact the principle,
3) you must be acting reasonably,
4) you must be actin gin the principles best interest.

## Employment Contracts

### Terms of employment

Employees are entitled a statement of service which is to be given to them within 2 months of their start date; there is no legal obligation on an employer to give an employee a contract. *Terms of Employment Information Act 1994-2014 states that:*
Terms can be reference where reasonable accessible to employee e.g. Company website, *Jones v Associated Tunnelling Ltd (1981)*

### Implied duties of the employer

Duty to pay wages
- On time, in full, allowances for deductions
- Amount to be agreed between parties
  - *National Minimum Wage Act 2000*
- Remuneration Method: *Payment of Wages Act 1991*

Duty to provide work where
- Linked to income, reputation, skills.  Constructive dismissal risk.
- No general obligation to provide work once paid

Duty to ensure safety
- Safe place/system of work, access to work, training, competent co-workers
- Indemnity for employee
- The employer must provide a safe place of work, free from bullying , harassment and stress; *Safety, Health and Welfare at Work Acts 2005 - 2010*

Duty to give paid holiday leave
- *Organisation of Working Time Act 1997*

Duty to treat employee with respect
*Spring v Guardian Assurance (1995)*

### Implied duty of the employee

- To be available for work
  - As specified in contract
  - Exception: Lawful industrial dispute
- To obey lawful orders and personal service
- To exercise care and skill in performance of their duties
- To exercise care and skill for their own and the safety of others
*Lister V Romford Ice&Cold Storage (1957)*
- Act in good faith & confidentiality in the interests of the employer

**Where an employee breaches any of the above duties, they are liable for any damage caused or arising from it**

## Contract of Services

### Control test

Does the employer control the time, place and mode of work, does the employer exert direct control on the employee. _Roche V Kelly (1969)_ (*if an employer tells a person not only what to do but how to do it, that the person will be considered to be an employee.*) _In re Sunday Tribune (1984) Tierney v An Post (2000)_

### Integration/organisation test

Is the worker an integral part of the business, do they attend board meeting, staff functions, given expenses etc. Are the workers work a core part of the business of Employer? _In re Sunday Tribune (1984)_

### Enterprise test

Can the worker get another person to fill in for them, i.e. can a driver get another driver to put their uniform on and drive their lorry with the client's logo on it and they "worker" go and do another job, if they can they are a self-employed contractor. working on own account or for 'employer', *" is the person who has engaged himself to perform these services performing them as a person in business on his own account"*

### Economic reality test.

Can they make money outside of the job, or go from one job to another, i.e. "a carpenter may go to several jobs through the day at their leisure, "they are self-employed", _Market Investigations v Minister for Social Security (1969)_ _In re Sunday Tribune (1984)_

### Contract for Services

Self-employed – not employees – do not satisfy the above tests

## Minimum wage Act

These are the hourly minimum rates of pay that are in force in Ireland since January 1st 2017.
1.   Experienced adult worker €9.25 per hour
2.   Over 18 and less than 2 years since first job €8.33
3.   Over 18 and less than 1 years since began first job €7.40
4.   Aged under 18   €6.48

## *Minimum Wage for Trainees:*

(Employee aged over 18, in structured training during working hours)
1st one third of course €6.94
2nd third of course €7.40
3rd part of course €8.33

## Employee leave

The *Organisation of Working Time Act 1997* provides that most employees are entitled to 4weeks annual holidays for each leave year with pro-rata entitlements for periods of employment of less than a year. In the case of employees working a normal 5 day week this would work out at 1 2/3 days per month worked or 20 days per annum.
Depending on time worked, employee's holiday entitlements should be calculated by one of the following methods:

- (i) 4 working weeks in a leave year in which the employee works at least 1,365 hours (unless it is a leave year in which he or she changes employment).
- (ii) 1/3 of a working week per calendar month that the employee works at least 117 hours.
- (iii) 8% of the hours an employee works in a leave year (but subject to a maximum of 4 working weeks).

## Termination of Employee Contract

- Agreement with notice (if no notice on the contract, statutory minimum notice applies)
- Death of employer/employee
- Frustration (see rules of frustration as below)
- Insolvency (or bankruptcy)
- Breach (one or both parties not adhering to the terms of employment)

## Dismissals

Unfair dismissal, this occurs when an employee is fired for an unfair reason such as age, race or religion, Wrongful dismissal, this occurs when a person is fired with NO NOTICE. Constructive dismissal, this happens when an employee feels they have no choice to leave because of their employer's behaviour. The **Unfair Dismissals Acts 1977 to 2016 states that:**

- <u>Any dismissal is presumed to be unfair </u>unless employer proves to the contrary
- Justified dismissal include lack of skill, lack of required qualifications, serious misconduct

- Unfair if wholly or partly from the listed grounds (please refer to your textbook)
- <u>Employers must also show acted reasonably</u>
- Employers required to have established grievance procedures and give written notice to employee of these procedures within 28 days of starting employment

## Disciplinary and Grievance Procedures

**Grievance** (a complaint an employee has regarding the terms and condition of their employment).

### Grievance procedure (suggested)

- The Grievance should be initially brought to the supervisors attention
- It this does not resolve the issue then it should be brought before the manager
- If still unresolved it goes to director
- Then to the workers reps/union
- Finally to the rights Commissioner/LRC/Labour Court/EAT

### Disciplinary Procedure (suggested)

**First steps**
- An oral warning
- A written warning
- A final written warning
- Suspension without pay
- Transfer to another are of the business
- Demotion
- Some other appropriate disciplinary action before considering dismissal

### Employee rights during the disciplinary process

1. Right to be advised in advance of a hearing
2. Right to know the <u>full</u> case against them
3. Right to respond
4. Right to representation
5. Investigation must be fair & impartial
6. Employee concerned & other relevant factors
7. Right to impartial appeal

## Multiple Choice Questions - Section 3 MCQs

1.    Sarah goes into a shop and sees a price label on a CD for €5. She takes the CD to the checkout, but the checkout operator tells her that the label is misprinted and should read €15. Sarah maintains that she only has to pay €5.
How would you describe the price on the label in terms of contract law?
      a) Sarah has a contract as the price is clearly stated
      b) Sarah has no contract, as this is an invitation to treat
      c) Sarah has no contract as she did not offer the store the €5
      d) None of the above

2.    Minimum wage in Ireland is:
      a) €9.25
      b) €8.64
      c) €8.50
      d) €11.50

3.    The case of ***Fisher v Bell*** in contract law dealt with
      a) Offers
      b) Invitations to treat
      c) Consideration
      d) Intention to Create Legal Relations

4.    Which of the following statements is/are correct?
      1. A term inserted into a contract attempting to exclude liability for damage to property caused by negligence is void unless it is reasonable.
      2. An exclusion clause which attempts to exclude liability for death or personal injury is void.
      a) 1 only
      b) 2 only
      c) Neither 1 nor 2
      d) Both 1 and 2

5.    James sent a letter to Sarah offering to sell Sarah his motorbike for €3,000. Sarah wrote back saying she accepted the offer and would pay in two instalments at the end of the two following months.
**Does Sarah have a contract with James?**
      a) No – because Sarah is trying to amend the terms.
      b) Yes – there has been an offer and acceptance and a binding contract exists
      c) No – Sarah's response constitutes a counter-offer and it voids the original offer.

d) Yes – Sarah's response is merely a clarification of contractual terms

6. Stan made an offer by letter posted which he posted on 15th January and delivered on 18th January. Jackie's reply accepting the offer was mailed on 19th January and the Stan received it on 20th January. Stan read the reply on 25th of January. **On which date was the contract made?**
   a) 15th January
   b) 18th January
   c) 19th January
   d) 25th January

7. Sam put his computer for sale in his shop window, the sign says *"special offer, computer for sale, €500.00"*. **Which of the following is correct?**
   a) This is an offer, and Sam must sell it to anyone who comes in and asks for it at that price.
   b) This is an invitation to treat only, as per Partridge v Crittenden
   c) This is an invitation to treat only, as per Fischer v Bell
   d) This is an offer as per Carlill v Carbolic Smokeball

8. Mary owed John €2,000. Mary's father, Thomas, agreed with John, in writing, to pay him €1,200 if he took it *"in full settlement"*. John took the €1,200 on this basis and then demanded €800.00 from Mary. Mary has refused to pay.
**Explain Mary's position?**
   a) Mary is liable – part payment of a debt is not consideration for a promise to discharge the debt
   b) Mary is not liable – part payment of a debt by a third party is good consideration for a promise not to sue for the balance
   c) Mary will be liable – Thomas, as her father, is not a third party
   d) Mary will not be liable – the agreement between John and Thomas was in writing

9. The law in relation to the "intention to create legal relations" in social and domestic situations, presumes that there is:
   1. An intention to create legal relations
   2. No intention to create legal relations
   3. An intention unless the presumption can be rebutted
   4. No intention unless it is in writing
      a) 1 and 2 only
      b) 1 and 3 only
      c) 2 and 4 only
      d) All of the above

10.   Steven is 25 years old, he has just started his first job after college, and he has not worked before this time. **Steven is entitled under the Payment of Wages Act to:**
  a) €9.25 ph.
  b) €7.40 ph.
  c) €6.48 ph.
  d) €8.33 ph.

11.   Jack has been working for 117 hours since he started working in his new job, he now requires a week off as holidays, **and how much holiday pay is Jack entitled to?**
  a) 2 working weeks
  b) 1/3 of a working week
  c) 9% of the total hours worked to date
  d) None of the above

12.   Susie offered to sell her car to Scott for €2,000 on January the 5th, Scott replied to this offer asking her if the car had been serviced and did it need new tyres. Susie replied on the 6th of January, it had new tyres and was serviced recently and said she would keep the offer open until the 10th of January. Scott contacted Susie on the 8th of January and told her he would give her €1,500 for the car, on the 9th of January, Jane bought the car from Susie. When Scott arrived to Susie's house on the 10th with €2,000, he was told it was sold. **Explain the legal position of Susie and Scott**
  a) There is a contract to sell at €2,000, so Scott may recover the car from Susie as it is now his property
  b) When Susie sold the car to Jane, she voided the contract with Scott
  c) There is an offer from Susie to sell to Scott for €2,000 which is still open until the 10th for Scott to accept
  d) There is no contract between Susie and Scott as Scott terminated the offer with Susie when he counter offered €1,500

13.   In which of the following circumstances is there an intention to create legal relations
  a) Taking your friends dog for a walk
  b) Taking your friends children to school, you have a contract are their paid child-minder
  c) Taking your friends children to school as a favour
  d) None of the above

14.   Jacob owes Andrew €1,000, this is to be paid by august the 1st, On July 15th Jacob send Andrew a cheque for €750.00 in *full and final payment* of the debt, Andrew lodged the cheque into his bank account, **explain If Andrew can sue Jacob for the €250.00**

a) Yes, since part payment of a debt cannot provide satisfaction for the agreement to
b) discharge the debt
c) No, because Andrew by his promise will be estopped from insisting on his legal rights
d) Yes, since the payment of €750.00 on the 15th of July is not adequate consideration for the promise not to sue
e) No, because part payment early at the request of Andrew provides satisfaction for the agreement to discharge the debt

15. **Which of the following statement are correct?**
 1. A condition is a term which is fundamental to the contract, the contract is void if a condition is breached
 2. A warranty is not fundamental to the contract, the contract is not void if a warranty is breached
 3. If an innominate term is broken the innocent party has the option whether or not to terminate the contract.
   a) 1 only
   b) 1 and 2 only
   c) 2 and 3 only
   d) 1, 2 and 3

16. **An unclear or ambiguous term in a contract is called:**
 a) Contra Proferentum and goes against the person relying on the contract
 b) Contra Proferentum and goes in favour of the person relying on the contract
 c) Volenti non fit injura and goes in favour of the person relying on it
 d) Unconscionable bargain and goes against the person replying on it

17. A contract which lacks legal formality is
 a) Void
 b) Voidable
 c) Unenforceable
 d) All of the above

18. Maria went to the cinema last week, she was queuing to get her ticket and noticed a sign over the counter in the cinema which stated, *management accept no liability for any injuries howsoever caused*, Maria tripped on a piece of carpet which was sticking up when she was leaving the cinema. **Explain Maria's legal position**
 a) She can bring a case for personal injury as she wasn't wearing her glasses and wasn't able to read the sign.

b) She cannot bring a personal injury case as the sign clearly stated in advance that the management accepted no liability
c) She can bring a personal injury case as no liability can be excluded for negligence
d) None of the above

19. Which of the follow does **not** allow the innocent party to repudiate the contract?
   a) A condition
   b) A warranty
   c) An innominate term
   d) None of the above

20. In terms of the law of contract, **which of the following statements is correct?**
   a) A breach of an innominate terms automatically voids the contract
   b) A breach of a warranty entitled the innocent part to repudiate the contract
   c) A breach of a condition automatically voids a contract
   d) A breach of a condition makes the contract voidable

21. Mikov, a wholesaler; orders 10 crates of lager with 24 bottles in each from his off licence, he receives all 240 bottles of lager, but in crates with different quantities in them. Mikov rejects the whole order, **what is Mikov's liability in contract law?**
   a) There is no breach of condition or warranty as this is not a consumer sale, therefore Mikov is liable for breach of contract
   b) There has only been a breach of warranty, therefore Mikov must pay and claim damages
   c) Mikov is in breach of contract by rejecting the goods and is liable to pay damages
   d) There has been a breach of condition that the goods match the description, therefore Mikov is entitled to treat the contract as discharged

22. **What does a breach of a condition entitle the injured party to do?**
   a) Claim damages only
   b) Sue on a quantum meruit
   c) Repudiate the contract and claim damages
   d) None of the above

23. Which of the following contracts would be enforceable by specific performance
   a) A plumber who has agreed to the terms of the contract and not started the job

b) A tiler who has started work and has had an accident leaving him out of work for a year
c) A minor
d) A contract for the payment of a deposit

24. Where the seller delivers goods which are **less** than the quantity ordered amount the buyer may:
   a) Either reject them or accept the short delivery and pay pro-rata for the goods that have been delivered
   b) Either reject or accept them. If he accepts them, he must pay the full contract price
   c) The buyer must reject the whole consignment
   d) The buyer must accept the whole consignment

25. Where the seller delivers goods which are **more** than the quantity ordered amount the buyer may:
   a) The buyer may accept the correct quantity and reject the remainder
   b) The buyer may accept the correct quantity and reject the remainder, OR may reject the entire delivery
   c) The buyer must accept the entire consignment
   d) The buyer must reject the entire consignment

26. The duty on a party to mitigate their losses means:
   a) They have a duty to ensure they get as much compensation as the law will allow
   b) They have a right to compensation for foreseeable damages caused
   c) They are required to reduce the impact and losses which they incur
   d) None of the above

27. Where there has been a breach of contract, the court must award one of the following:
   a) Specific performance
   b) Damages
   c) Injunctions
   d) All of the above

28. What is the equitable remedy of recession?
   a) The contract never existed
   b) Changes to the contract
   c) Compensation to the injured party
   d) None of the above

29. The court in the case of **Stilk v Myrich** ruled that:
    a) No extra consideration was given by the crew, therefore no money was payable
    b) Extra consideration was given as the crew had come back with the ship as promised
    c) Consideration was given as the they were promised the money
    d) None of the above

30. In the case of **Hartley v Ponsoby** the court ruled:
    a) No extra consideration was given by the crew, therefore no money was payable
    b) Extra consideration was given as the crew; they had done extra work and gone beyond their contractual duties.
    c) Consideration was given as the they were promised the money
    d) None of the above

31. Intention to create legal relation in the case of **Edwards v Skyways**, was
    a) Proven as intention is implied in commercial contracts, even if signed otherwise
    b) Not proven, as there was no intention as Edwards had signed a contract station it was "ex gratia" and no intention existed
    c) Edwards had signed a contract stating there was no intention, this inserted an exclusion clause
    d) None of the above

32. The Enterprise test in defining whether a worker is as employee or self-employed contractor investigates:
    1. If the employer decides the hours and place of work of the employee
    2. If the worker has to attend meetings and is given expenses to cover diesel or petrol
    3. If the worker is allowed to work for other companies while worker for employer.
    4. If the worker has the power to instruct another worker to take over their job on their behalf.
        a) 1 only
        b) 1 and 4
        c) 3 and 4
        d) 2 and 3

33. The control test in defining if a worker is employed or self-employed is defined:
    a) If the employer decides the hours and place of work of the employee

b) If the worker has to attend meetings and is given expenses to cover diesel or petrol
c) If the worker is allowed to work for other companies while worker for employer.
d) If the worker has the power to instruct another worker to take over their job on their behalf.

34.    When defining consideration in a contract, which of the following is **not** good consideration
1. A father telling his son he will pay him to stop complaining,
2. A son promising to stop complaining if his father pays him money
3. A son asking his father how much is it worth for him to stop complaining
4. None of the above
   a. 1 only
   b. 1 and 2 only
   c. 1, 2 and 3
   d. 1 and 3 only

35.    The case of **Whyte v Bluett** concerned
a) A self-employed contractor claiming he was an employee
b) A father offering to pay his son to stop complaining
c) A son offering to stop complaining if he got paid
d) A worker who was defined as self-employed as he could get another worker to take his place

36.    Which case defined the principle that where a party provides more than an existing duty requires them to do; they can look for extra payment?
a) Whyte v Bluett
b) Fischer v Bell
c) Edwards v Skyways
d) Glasbrook Bros v Glamorgan City Council

37.    In the case of **Harvella Investments v Royal Trust Company** the courts stated that:
a) A price need not be agreed in order for referential bids to be accepted
b) Referential bids are not acceptable, as a price needs to be stated
c) Referential bids are not legally binding
d) None of the above

38.    An implied contract is one where:
a) The parties must state the terms of the contract
b) The terms do not need to be written down, they can be unspoken, unwritten

    c) Silence does not constitute acceptance
    d) None of the above

39. The case of **Spurling v Bradshaw** defined the principle that
    a) A contract is void if it is signed after the agreement is made
    b) A contract is valid even if it is signed after the agreement is made
    c) A contract is valid if it is signed after it is made, as long as the parties have previous dealings
    d) A contract is not valid if it is signed after it is made, even if the parties have previous dealings

40. When one party to a contract states before it starts that they will not be able to perform the contract his breach is called
    a) Anticipatory breach
    b) Repudiatory breach
    c) Liquidated breach
    d) Fundamental breach

41. Motorway Builder Ltd agreed to build a new road for XCity to be completed on 15 March 2017. The contract provided for a penalty of €1,000 per day from 15 March to date of actual completion.
The road was 20 days late and as a result XCity was able to prove that they had lost
€60,000 of revenue and €5,000 of profits in the St Patrick 's Day period.
**What is the maximum amount XCity may recover from Motorway Builder Ltd?**
    a) Nil
    b) €20,000
    c) €50,000
    d) €65,000

42. What is the Statute of Limitation for breach of a simple contract?
    a) 1 year
    b) 2 years
    c) 3 years
    d) 6 years

43. Michael, an estate agent in Dublin has on his books two houses for sale, Mark isn't sure which one to buy as he likes both of them, he reads the brochures for both houses and decided to go with house B, as the garden in house B is bigger than the garden of house A. The brochure states that the garden in house A is 30m x 10m and the garden in house B is 40m x 10m, both houses are in the same street and house B is 5k cheaper. Michael goes to view house B, but it is dark and he only looks into the garden, and doesn't measure it, he buys house B and subsequently finds out that the

garden is in fact 30m x 10 m and not 40m x 10m as stated in the brochure, he is considering suing the estate agent, he asks for your advice. **Explain to Michael if the wrong size in the brochure was a:**

   a) Condition
   b) Warranty
   c) Representation
   d) Innominate term

44.   A common mistake occurs when
   a) Both parties are mistaken about different terms in the contract
   b) Both parties are mistaken about the same term in the contract
   c) One party is mistaken concerning facts in the contract
   d) None of the above

45.   Dan has just given you notice of his intention not to renew his tenancy, you go to the house and realise there is a lot of damage done to the property, you have not been to the house in over two years to inspect it and so you are not sure when the damage occurred, you have decided to bring a case against Dan for damages done to the house, **when does the Stature of Limitations run out on damage to property?**

   a) 1 year from the date you discover it
   b) 2 years from the date you discover it
   c) 3 years from the last date you inspected the property
   d) 6 years from the date the damage occurred.

46.   The court ruled in the case of ***Hadley v Baxendale*** that:
   a) losses which arise naturally from the breach of contract.
   b) losses which are in both parties contemplation which would probably arise from the breach.
   c) losses which arise naturally from the breach of contract or which are in both parties contemplation as a probable result of its breach.
   d) losses which are reasonably foreseen by both parties at the time the contract is made are recoverable.

47.   Sam has worked for her employer for 3 years, she wants to leave her job, at the same time her employer is considering giving Sam notice to leave, her contract states that she and the employer must give the statutory minimum notice, advise Sam of the required notice she must give,

   a) One week
   b) Two weeks
   c) Four weeks
   d) Eight weeks

48.   Which one of the following is not a remedy available where an employee wins a case for unfair dismissal?

a) Compensation
b) Re-instatement
c) Re-engagement
d) Specific performance

49. Which of the following statements are correct?
1) An employer is vicariously liable for the torts committed by employees in the course of their employment.
2) An employer is vicariously liable for the torts committed by their self-employed contractors in the course of their contracts.
    a) 1 only
    b) 2 only
    c) 1 and 2
    d) None

50. Which ONE of the following is normally implied into a contract of employment?
    a) The employer's duty to provide a reference
    b) The employees duty to follow all instructions
    c) The employer's duty to provide work
    d) The employer's duty to pay wages

Section 4 – LO4 – Consumer Law

### *Caveat Emptor*

*"let the buyer beware" Doctrine of Caveat Emptor.*
Caveat emptor is a Latin expression which means buyers beware. In the ordinary course of buying goods the buyer should satisfy themselves as to the quality of the goods they are buying, and take the consequences for not looking at what they were getting. It is no part of the seller's duty to point out the defects in the goods he is selling.
Exemptions: - However, the rule of caveat emptor will not apply under the following circumstances.
1. Where the buyer relies upon the skill and judgment of the seller
2. Where the sale is under patent or trade name
3. Merchantability
4. Seller is guilty of fraud: A contract of sale of goods must satisfy all essentials of valid contract and therefore if the consent of the buyer was obtained by fraud, the seller is not protected by the doctrine of caveat emptor. Similarly if the seller knowingly conceals any defect in the goods which the buyer could not discover on a reasonable examination the doctrine of caveat emptor shall not apply.

*Consumer, defined*

S3 of the SGSSA 1980, defines a consumer as a party who;

- *is not making the contract in the course of business*
- *uses the goods/services are for ordinarily private use*
- *buys the goods from a seller acting in the course of business*

### Sales contracts distinguished from other contracts

The contract for the sale of goods must be distinguished from other contracts; this is because many other contracts resemble sales contracts, when in fact they are not. Such as:
a contract of barter or exchange
a gift
a contract of bailment
a contract of hire-purchase
a contract of loan on the
security of goods
a contract for the supply of services
a contract of agency, and
licences of intellectual property such as 'sales' of computer software.

*The SGSSA covers the Sale of goods*

## Goods are defined as;
"all chattels personal other than things in action and money".
'Things in action' ('choses in action') include debts, shares, patents, cheques, bills of exchange and promissory notes.

***SGSSA 1980, Section 2 (4):*** Where ownership or the 'property' is transferred immediately from the seller to the buyer, this contract is called a contract for **'sale'.**
***SGSSA 1980, Section 2 (5):*** Where ownership is to be transferred at some future time, this contract is called an **'agreement to sell'.**

**Consumer law** – *The Sale of Goods and supply of Services Act 1893-1980*

***S12 Good title,*** seller owns it or has permission to sell it. *Rowland V Divell (1923)*
- Implied Condition that <u>seller has a right to sell the goods</u>
- Free of any rights or interference by third parties

***S13 Fit description***, if you are buying something which is 100% wool then you expect to get it. *T O'Regan & Sons Ltd v. Micro-Bio (Irl) Ltd, 1980.* and *Arcos Ltd vs. Ronaasen*[1]
- Must correspond with description, **even where sample** provided and match sample
- Exception **'bought as seen'** – EXPRESS TERM

***S14 merchantable quality***, getting moneys worth, if you are paying for something you want to be able to get good use, if you buy a cheap item you would expect it to be less quality considering the price you pay. *McCullough Sales Ltd v. Chetham Timber Co. Ltd, 1983*
- of a **reasonable standard**
- suitable for the purpose(s) for which goods of that kind are **commonly bought**
- as **durable** as is reasonable to expect having regard to any description applied to them, the price (if relevant), and all other relevant circumstances.

***S14 fit for purpose***, a waterproof rain coat that lets rain in is NOT a raincoat, is may be water resist, check the label. *Priest V. Last*[2]

---

[1] Arcos Ltd vs. Ronaasen, the sellers sold a quantity of wooden stoves to the buyers. The thickness was given as half an inch. When the goods were delivered the arbitration found that only five per cent were half an inch thick.

- **goods in course of a business** and
- buyer makes known, expressly or by implication, to the seller
- **any particular purpose** for which the goods are being bought, then there is implied condition
- that goods are **reasonable fit for that purpose**, whether or not that is a purpose for which such goods are commonly supplied

**S15, sale by sample**, if you go to Argos and order a white 1200 spin, you should get just that, not another colour and spin. *Nichol v. Godts (1854)*
- Goods will correspond with the sample
- Buyer will have reasonable opportunity to compare the goods with the sample
- The goods free of any defect making them merchantable that not apparent on reasonable inspection of the sample

---

[2] In Priest vs. Last (1930) 2 K.B. 148, it was held that the purpose of a hot water bottle was made known by implication. If the purpose is obvious as in case of single purpose goods, nothing need be said.

### *Nemo dat quod non habet*

No one can give what they do not have. A person cannot transfer a better title than they have themselves. *See above, good title.*

***Caveat Emptor (Let the buyer beware)*** *Common law principle that buyer through examination of goods can determine the quality and fitness for purpose purchased*

## Market Overt

An open public market, at market specific times, authorised and regulated by law at which purchasers of goods with certain exceptions acquire good title regardless of any defects in the seller's title. There is a requirement that the buyer buys in "good faith"( done honestly, whether done negligently or not)

## Transfer of Property as between Seller and Buyer.

### Goods must be ascertained (identified)

If there is a contract for the sale of unascertained goods, no property in the goods is transferred to the buyer unless and until the goods are ascertained (Goods identified and agreed upon at that time a contract of sale is made, "example: Sarah sells her motorcycle bearing registration number 131 D XXXX")

### Rules as to the Intentions of the parties

**18. (1)** Property passes when intended to pass (2) The terms of the contract, the conduct of the parties, and the circumstances of the case will define the intention of the parties.
**19.** Unless a different intention appears the following ascertaining are **rules** for ascertaining the intention of the parties as to the times at which the property in the goods is to pass to the buyer.

**Rule 1.**—Where there is an unconditional contract for the sale of specific goods, in a deliverable state, the property in the goods passes to the buyer when the contract is made, and it is immaterial whether the time of payment or the time of delivery, or both, be postponed. [34]

---

[3] Goods that in the state that the buyer would under the contract BE BOUND to take delivery of them

**Rule 2**.—Where there is a contract for the sale of specific goods and the seller is bound to do something to the goods, for the purpose of putting them into a deliverable state, the property does not pass until such thing be done, and the buyer has notice thereof. S. 15 [No. 71.] Sale of Goods Act 1893 [1893.] [5]

**Rule 3**.—Where there is a contract for the sale of specific goods in a deliverable state, but the seller is bound to weigh, measure, test, or do some other act or thing with reference to the goods for the purpose of ascertaining the price, the property does not pass until such act or thing be done, and the buyer has notice thereof.

**Rule 4**.—When goods are delivered to the buyer on approval or "on sale or return" or other similar terms the property therein passes to the buyer:— (a) When he signifies his approval or acceptance to the seller or does any other act adopting the transaction:
(b) If he does not signify his approval or acceptance to the seller but retains the goods without giving notice of rejection, then, if a time has been fixed for the return of the goods, on the expiration of such time, and, if no time has been fixed, on the expiration of a reasonable time. What is a reasonable time is a question of fact.

**Rule 5.—(1)** Where there is a contract for the sale of unascertained or future goods by description, and goods of that description and in a deliverable state are unconditionally appropriated to the contract, either by the seller with the assent of the buyer, or by the buyer with the assent of the seller, the property in the goods thereupon passes to the buyer. Such assent may be express or implied, and may be given either before or after the appropriation is made.

---

[4] Where the seller bound to weigh, measure, test or do something for the purpose of ascertaining the price of the goods, the property does not pass to the buyer until such thing is done by the seller, and the buyer has notice/knowledge of it

[5] In **Underwood Ltd v Burgh Castle Brick and Cement Syndicate**, a contract was made for the sale 'free on rail' of an engine weighing thirty tons. At the time the contract was made, the engine was fixed to the floor of the plaintiff's premises and had to be separated from its base and dismantled before it could be delivered. The engine was damaged while being loaded onto a railway truck. **COA Held**: The engine was not in a deliverable state.

### Risk passes with property

**20.** (1) Unless otherwise agreed, the goods remain at the seller's risk until the property in them is transferred to the buyer, but when the property in them is transferred to the buyer the goods are at the buyer's risk, whether delivery has been made or not.

### Sale by person not owner

**21.** (1) Subject to this Act, if goods are sold by a person who is not the owner of them, and who does not sell them under the authority or with the consent of the owner, the buyer acquires no better title to the goods than the seller had, unless the owner's conduct precludes the owner from denying the seller's authority to sell. [6](if a person buys goods from a person who does not have the right to sell them they

### Market overt

**22.** (1) Where goods are sold in market overt, according to the usage of the market, *(in law this is usually sunrise to sunset)* the buyer acquires a good title to the goods, provided he buys them in good faith and without notice of any defect or want of title on the part of the seller. (bought outside these times they are liable for prosecution)

### Sale under voidable title

**23.** When the seller of goods has a voidable title to them, but the seller's title has not been avoided at the time of the sale, the buyer acquires a good title to the goods, if they are bought in good faith and without notice of the seller's defect of title.

### Revesting of property in stolen goods on conviction of offender

**24.** (1) If goods have been stolen and the offender is prosecuted to conviction, the property in the goods stolen revests in the person who was the owner of the goods, or that person's personal representative, despite any intermediate dealing with them, whether by sale in market overt or otherwise.

### Seller or buyer in possession after sale

**25.** (1) If a person having sold goods continues or is in possession of the goods, or of the documents of title to the goods, the delivery or transfer by

---

[6] if the goods or documents are in the person's actual custody or are held by another who is subject to the person's control or for the person or on the person's behalf

that person, or by a mercantile agent acting for that person, of the goods or documents of title under any sale, pledge or other disposition of them, or under any agreement for the sale, pledge or other disposition of them, to any person receiving the same in good faith and without notice of the previous sale has the same effect as if the person making the delivery or transfer were expressly authorized by the owner of the goods to make the delivery or transfer. (2) Subsection (1) does not apply to a sale, pledge or other disposition of

a) goods, or

b) documents of title to goods, other than negotiable documents of title,

## Performance of the Contract

### *Duties of seller and buyer*

**27.** It is the duty of the seller to deliver the goods, and of the buyer to accept and pay for them, in accordance with the terms of the contract of sale.

### *Payment and delivery are concurrent conditions*

**28.** Unless otherwise agreed, delivery of the goods and payment of the price are concurrent conditions; that is to say, the seller must be ready and willing to give possession of the goods to the buyer in exchange for the price, and the buyer must be ready and willing to pay the price in exchange for possession of the goods.

### *Rules as to delivery*

**29.**—(1) Whether it is for the buyer to take possession of the goods or for the seller to send them to the buyer is a question depending in each case on the contract, express or implied, between the parties. Apart from any such contract, express or implied, the place of delivery is the seller's place of business, if he have one, and if not, his residence: Provided that, if the contract be for the sale of specific goods, which to the knowledge of the parties when the contract is made are in some other place, then that place is the place of delivery.[7]

---

[7] If the contract involves delivery to a carrier, once the seller delivers the goods to the buyer or to the carrier for the purpose of transmission (delivery) to the buyer. The seller is deemed too have an unconditionally appropriated the goods to the contract.

### Time of Delivery

Where under the contract of sale the seller is bound to send the goods to the buyer, but NO TIME for sending them is fixed, the seller is bound to send them within a **reasonable time**

### Delivery of wrong quantity

**30** Where the Seller delivers to the buyer a quantity of goods **less than that which he contracted** to sell:-
   a) the buyer may reject all the goods so delivered, or[8]
   b) if the buyer accepts the goods so delivered, he is bound to pay for them at the contract rate

Where the Seller delivers to the buyer a **larger quantity of goods than that which he contracted** to sell, the buyer may:-
   a) Accept the goods included in the contract & reject the rest; or
   b) Reject all the goods
   c) Accept all the goods. (if buyer accepts all the goods, he has to pay for the goods at the contract rate)

Where the Seller delivers to the buyer the goods he contracted to sell **mixed with goods of a different description not included in the contract**, the buyer may:-
   a) Accept the goods which are in accordance with the contract & reject the rest; or
   b) Reject the whole delivery.

---

[8] Harland & Wolff Ltd v J. Burstall & Co. the contract was for 500 loads of timber.
**Held**: that delivery of 470 loads would have been non-performance of the contract entitling buyer to reject

## Instalment deliveries

**31** (1) Unless otherwise agreed, the buyer of goods is not bound to accept delivery by instalments. (2) If there is a contract for the sale of goods to be delivered by stated instalments, which are to be separately paid for, and the seller makes defective deliveries in respect of one or more instalments, or the buyer neglects or refuses to take delivery of or pay for one or more instalments, it is a question in each case depending on the terms of the contract and the circumstances of the case whether the breach of contract is
   a) a repudiation of the whole contract, or
   b) a severable breach giving rise to a claim for compensation but not to a right to treat the whole contract as repudiated.

## Delivery to carrier

Delivery means voluntary transfer of possession from one person to another. Constructive delivery is sufficient.(*need not include physical transfer*)
**32** (1) If, in pursuance of a contract of sale, the seller is authorized or required to send the goods to the buyer, delivery of the goods to a carrier, whether named by the buyer or not, for transmission to the buyer is deemed, unless there is evidence to the contrary, to be a delivery of the goods to the buyer.[9]

## Acceptance

**35.** The buyer is deemed to have accepted the goods when
   a) the buyer intimates to the seller that the buyer has accepted them,
   b) the goods have been delivered to the buyer, and the buyer does any act in relation to them which is inconsistent with the ownership of the seller, or
   c) after the lapse of a reasonable time, the buyer retains the goods without intimating to the seller that the buyer has rejected them.

---

[9] Place of delivery – whether the seller is required to send the goods to the buyer or the buyer has to take possession of the goods depends on what has been agreed upon between them.

### *Buyer not bound to return rejected goods*

**36.** Unless otherwise agreed, if goods are delivered to the buyer and the buyer refuses to accept them, having the right so to do, the buyer is not bound to return them to the seller, but it is sufficient if the buyer intimates to the seller that the buyer refuses to accept them.

### *Liability of buyer for neglecting or refusing to take delivery of goods*

**37.** (1) When the seller is ready and willing to deliver the goods, and requests the buyer to take delivery, and the buyer does not within a reasonable time after the request take delivery of the goods, the buyer is liable to the seller for[10]

a) any loss occasioned by the buyer's neglect or refusal to take delivery, and

b) a reasonable charge for the care and custody of the goods.

---

[10] If the Buyer refused or neglect to take delivery, the buyer would be liable for any loss due to his own refusal or negligence

Rights of Unpaid Seller Against the Goods

### *Unpaid seller and seller rights*

**39.** (1) In this Part, **"seller"** includes any person who is in the position of a seller, as, for instance, an agent of the seller to whom the bill of lading has been endorsed, or a consignor or agent who has himself or herself paid or is directly responsible for the price.

### *Unpaid seller's rights*

**40.** (1) Subject to this or any other Act, even if the property in the goods may have passed to the buyer, the unpaid seller of goods, as such, has by implication of law[11]
(a) a lien on the goods or right to retain them for the price while the seller is in possession of them,
(b) in case of the insolvency of the buyer, a right of stopping the goods in transit after the seller has parted with the possession of them, and
(c) a right of resale as limited by this Act.

### *Unpaid seller's lien*

**41.** (1) Subject to this Act, the unpaid seller of goods who is in possession of them is entitled to retain possession of them until payment or tender of the price in the following cases:
(a) if the goods have been sold without any stipulation as to credit;
(b) if the goods have been sold on credit, but the term of credit has expired;
(c) if the buyer becomes insolvent.
(2) The seller may exercise the right of lien even if the seller is in possession of the goods as agent or bailee for the buyer.

---

[11] If the buyer failed to pay for the price of the goods, the seller may sue the buyer for the price when:
The property in goods (ownership) has passed to the buyer; or
The price is payable on a certain day but the buyer failed to pay on that day; irrespective of delivery, or the property in the goods has not passed to the buyer

### Part delivery

**42.** An unpaid seller who has made part delivery of the goods may exercise the right of lien or retention on the remainder, unless that part delivery has been made under circumstances that show an agreement to waive the lien or right of retention.

### Termination of lien

**43.** (1) The unpaid seller of goods loses the lien or right of retention
(a) when the seller delivers the goods to a carrier or other bailee for transmission to the buyer without reserving the right of disposal of the goods,
(b) when the buyer or the buyer's agent lawfully obtains possession of the goods, and
(c) by waiver of it.

### Right to stop goods in transit[12] (Stoppage in Transit)

**44.** Subject to this Act, when the buyer of goods becomes insolvent, the unpaid seller who has parted with the possession of the goods has the right of stopping them in transit; that is to say, the unpaid seller may resume possession of the goods as long as they are in course of transit, and may retain them until payment or tender of the price. This can happen when the buyer becomes insolvent, and when the goods are in control of a carrier (in transit). An insolvent seller is a person who has ceased to pay his debts in the ordinary course of business, or cannot pay his debts as they become due, whether he has committed an act of bankruptcy or not. [13]

### How stoppage in transitu is affected.

**46.** (1) The unpaid seller may exercise the right of stoppage in transit
   a) by taking actual possession of the goods, or
   b) by giving notice of the seller's claim to the carrier, or other bailee in whose possession the goods are.

---

[12] Goods are deemed to be in the course of transit ; from the time when they are delivered to a carrier or other bailee for the purpose of transmission to the buyer, or until the buyer or his agent in that behalf takes delivery of them from such carrier or other bailee.
[13] This is a right of an unpaid seller to stop the goods in transit, to resume possession of the goods as long as they are in the course of transit. The seller may retain the goods until payment of the price

## Actions for Breach of the Contract

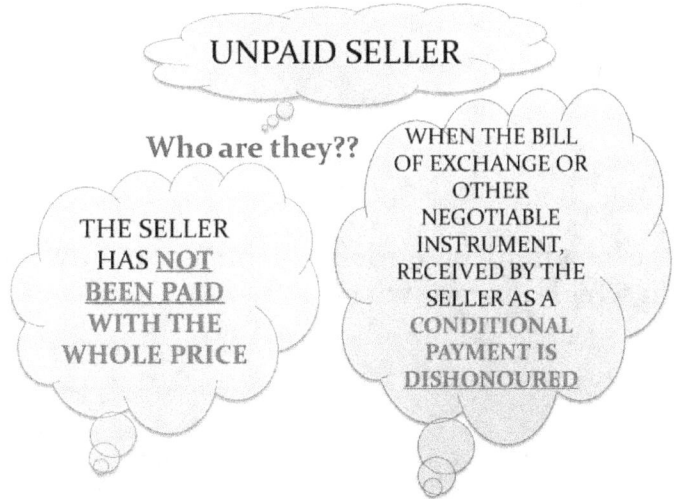

## Action for price

**49** (1) If, under a contract of sale, the property in the goods has passed to the buyer, and the buyer wrongfully neglects or refuses to pay for the goods according to the terms of the contract, the seller may maintain an action against the buyer for the price of the goods.

## Damages for nonacceptance

**50** (1) If the buyer wrongfully neglects or refuses to accept and pay for the goods, the seller may maintain an action against the buyer for damages for nonacceptance.

## Damages for nondelivery

**51** (1) If the seller wrongfully neglects or refuses to deliver the goods to the buyer, the buyer may maintain an action against the seller for damages for nondelivery.

## Specific performance

**52** (1) In any action for breach of contract to deliver specific or ascertained goods, the court may, if it thinks fit, on the application of the plaintiff, order that the contract be performed specifically without giving the defendant the option of retaining the goods on payment of damages.

## Interest and special damages

**54** This Act does not affect the right of the buyer or the seller to recover interest or special damages in any case where by law interest or special damages may be recoverable, or to recover money paid if the consideration for the payment of it has failed.

## Consumer Protection Act 2007

## Misleading practices

Telling lies (about the product) or enticing a buyer to buy by telling them things about the item which are not true.

## Aggressive Practices

Enticing (*pressuring by words or actions*) a customer with lies about the business, such as competition with no prizes, not leaving a customer's home or pressuring them into buying goods, saying your shop is shutting down etc., (*if you see a closing down sign this might entice you in to see if you can get a bargain, if there is no closing down sale then this means they have pressured you into making a choice you might not have made*)

## The Consumer Protection Act 2007 (CPA)

Consumers are entitled to avail of the law to protect their rights and an interest, the **Consumer Protection act 2007** is just such a piece of law. Consumers are protected from providers who try to be misleading by providing false, misleading and deceptive information. Misleading advertising, misleading information and withholding material information are considered misleading practices, Providers are also prohibited from aggressive or prohibited practices such as harassment, coercion, or exercising undue influence. Examples of harassment are pressurising, intimidating and taking advantage of vulnerable consumers.
(**Example:** *Misleading could a lie about the product, weight, price, origin, handmade, manmade, the ingredients etc. Aggressive could be about the selling of the product, how they sell the product i.e. a shop putting up closing down sales, these are illegal unless the shop is actually shutting down, it may force a buy to make a decision they might not otherwise have made, or a salesperson refusing to leave the home of a resident, or pyramid schemes etc.*)

## Functions of National Consumer Agency

The main functions of the NCA are to:
1. Inform consumers of their rights through consumer information
2. Promote a strong consumer culture through consumer education and awareness

3. Help businesses comply with consumer law through its enforcement activities, and,
4. Represent consumer interests at all levels of local and national consumer policy development through targeted research and forceful advocacy

## Powers of National Consumer Agency

1. To advise and make recommendations on any legislation or policy which is likely to impact on consumer protection
2. To make proposals for new legislation
3. To appoint authorised officers to enforce consumer legislation. These officers have the right to enter premises, get documentation and other evidence in relation to any trade or business which is being investigated. They have the right to be accompanied by the Gardaí, if necessary and apply to the courts for search warrants

Under **the Consumer Protection Act, 2007** it is a an offence for any retailer, service provider, manufacturer or advertiser to make a false or misleading claim about themselves, (*they are a member of a registered governing body etc.*), or to make any false representations about or goods, services or prices

## Supply of Services

The supply of services does not extend to the employer/employee contract. Under S.39 implies terms into contracts where the supplier is offering a service in the course of his or her business.

These include, that:

(a) that the supplier has the <u>necessary skill</u> to render the service;
(b) that the supplier will supply the services with <u>due skill, care and diligence;</u>
(c) that, where <u>materials</u> are used, they will be <u>sound and reasonably fit for the purpose</u> for which they are required
(d) that, where goods are supplied under the contract of service, they will be of <u>merchantable quality</u> (S.39)

The parties may exclude these terms from a contract for the supply of services by:

- The express agreement of the parties.
- A course of dealing indicates that those terms are normally excluded.
- It is customary in the relevant trade to exclude these terms and this is known or ought to be known by both parties.

However, where the supplier of the service is dealing with consumers, they may not exclude liability which is unfair or unjust, and the consumer must be made aware of the exclusion clauses at the time to the formation of the contract.

## Multiple Choice Questions - Section Four - LO 4 MCQs

1.  The case of **Rowland v Divall (1923)** defined was brought under which
    Section 12(1)of the Sale of Goods and Supply of Services Act 1980
    a)      Good title
    b)      Fit for purpose
    c)      Merchantable quality
    d)      Fits the description

2.  The terms of the sale of Goods and Supply of Services are defined in the
    a)  Sale of goods and Supply of Services Act 1981
    b)  Sale of goods and Supply of Services Act 1990
    c)  Sale of goods and Supply of Services Act 1980
    d)  Sale of goods and Supply of Services Act 1880

3.  Under **Section 27 of the SGSSA 1980** if agreed, there is an obligation on the
    seller to deliver the goods to the buyer.
    a)      true
    b)      false

4.  **Section 12(2) of the SGSSA 1980** states that:
    a)      The seller must inform the buyer of any incumbrances
    b)      The buyer must ask if there are any incumbrances
    c)      There goods must be free from any incumbrances
    d)      The goods can have an incumbrance so long as the buyer agrees
            to them at the time of purchase

5.      Stoppage in transit refers to:
    a)      The driver delivering the goods to the specified buyer must do so
            without stopping
    b)      The seller can stop the goods which have already been shipped
            to the buy should they become insolvent
    c)      The goods can be stopped if the seller realises that the buyer
            cannot pay for them (goes into liquidation)
    d)      The buyer can request that the goods can be stopped in transit,
            and be returned to the seller as they can't afford them.

6.  The onus of proof in a claim for defective products is
    a)  On the seller
    b)  The manufacturer

c) The consumer

d) The public

7. The seller can only transfer such rights as they possess
   a) Yes, the seller can only transfer such rights as they possess
   b) Yes only if agreed by both parties at the time of the sale
   c) No, the buyer has no right to possession unless transferred by the seller
   d) No, only if the buyer can prove they bought it in good faith

8. Ownership passes when the contract is made, if:
   a) the goods reached the buy in a reasonable time
   b) the goods were of satisfactory quality
   c) the goods were as stated in the agreement
   d) if the goods are in a deliverable state

9. If the goods are not in a deliverable state, ownership passes when:
   a) the buyer informs the seller that the goods are not in a deliverable state
   b) when the goods have been put in such state, and the buyer has been informed
   c) when the goods are delivered
   d) then the buyer asks for them to be delivered

10. If the goods must be weighed or measured by the seller, ownership passes
    once
    a) the seller informs the buyer that they are the correct weight
    b) the goods have been weighed or measured and the seller informed
    c) the buy informs the seller they do not need the goods weighted any more
    d) the seller makes an informed guess as to the weight of the goods

11. A defective product is one that
    a) Has holes in it
    b) Is not fit for purpose
    c) One that is not merchantable quality
    d) Fails to provide safety which a person is entitled to expect

12. Where the goods are sold *"on approval"* the ownership passes once the:
    a) seller approved the deliver
    b) seller crosses out the approval requirement on the contract

    c)      buyer believes the seller when they said the goods were in good condition

    d)      when the buyer approves the goods and after a reasonable time.

13.    If specific goods perish after a contract is made, but before delivery, the

            contract is:
    a)      void
    b)      voidable
    c)      unenforceable
    d)      frustrated

14.    What does 'nemo dat quod non habet' mean?
    a)      no one can give that which he has not got
    b)      seller cannot sell if they are under 18
    c)      the seller must confirm the weight and measurements
    d)      no one can sell which he does not own

15.    HACCP is the anagram for the
    a)      Hot and cold central point
    b)      Hazard analysis and critical control points
    c)      Hazard and critical control points
    d)      Hazard area control and chilled points

16.    What are the rules in regarding to sale prices
    a)      Advertised in the same store for one week previous
    b)      Been advertised in any chain store for 28 days in the last three months
    c)      Been advertised in the same store for 28 days in the last three months
    d)      Been advertised at a higher price for more than 28 days

17.    If a delivery time is agreed,
    a)      the delivery must be in a reasonable time
    b)      time is assumed to be of the essence
    c)      the delivery is implied to be within one day
    d)      time can be changed with the agreement of the seller and courier

18.    If the buyer fails to take delivery within a reasonable time they are:
    a)      entitled to return the goods to the buyer
    b)      have the goods at a cheaper price
    c)      liable for any loss
    d)      liable for the sellers restocking fees

19. If the price of the goods is not agreed at the time of delivery, the buy must
    pay:
    a)   whatever price is on the invoice
    b)   a reasonable price
    c)   a reasonable price depending on the market conditions and condition of the goods
    d)   the price which the buy believes they are worth

20. Misleading advertising is
    a)   When a consumer is happy with the items as advertised on the radio
    b)   When a seller knowingly makes false claims
    c)   When the advertisement is for children's toys before 7pm
    d)   A consumer wishes to make a seller have catalogues printed

21. The buyer may reject the entire delivery if the amount is more or less than
    agreed, however:
    a)   minute deviations won't apply
    b)   deviations must be within industry standards
    c)   the seller can insist that the buy take deliver
    d)   the buyer can demand the seller come and take the extra away or bring more if the delivery is less than agreed

22. The function of the Competition and consumer Protection Agency
    a)   To provide information to sellers to ensure they can get away with prohibited practices
    b)   To investigate sellers who are not adhering to the CPA 2007
    c)   To promote ways in which consumers can bring the sellers to the small claims court
    d)   To keep an eye on prices so that sellers know their competitors markets

23. Buyers don't have to accept delivery by instalments unless;
    a)   previously agreed by both parties
    b)   the buyer was unsure if they wanted instalments at the time of purchase
    c)   the seller contacted them and told them they were obliged to
    d)   both parties believed the other would agree to it

24. The case of **Priest v Last** involved
    a)   section 12 SGSSA 1980
    b)   section 13 SGSSA 1980
    c)   section 14 SGSSA 1980
    d)   section 15 SGSSA 1980

25. The buyer has no duty to return rejected goods
    a) true
    b) false

26. Prohibited practices are actions such as
    a) Misappropriate claims
    b) Aggressive practices
    c) Adamant claims
    d) product development

27. An agreement to prevent the right to examine goods is;
    a) allowable on the agreement of both parties
    b) not allowed under any circumstances
    c) allowed on the acceptance of the buyer
    d) not allowed unless the court determines otherwise

28. A buyer can sue for damages for breach of a condition or warranty, but;
    a) can only reject the goods for a breach of a warranty
    b) can only reject the goods for fraudulent misrepresentation
    c) can only reject the goods for a breach of condition
    d) cannot reject the goods, but must instigate legal action

29. An aggressive practice is one that
    a) Entices a seller into a contract
    b) allows the buyers to decide freely their purchases
    c) Allows sellers to provide false information
    d) Misleads buyers as to the geographical origin or the goods

30. A Lien is the seller's right to;
    a) withhold delivery as long as they still have possession
    b) stop the goods in transit and have them returned
    c) sue the buyer for non-acceptance
    d) have the goods diverted to another buyer for resale

31. The seller has a right to resell if the goods are perishable, or if notice is given;
    a) when a buyer agrees to the resale
    b) fails to pay within a reasonable time
    c) the seller gets higher offer from the new buyer
    d) the seller believes the buyer cannot pay for the goods

32. A misleading practice is one that
    a) Helps consumers to identify lying sellers
    b) Tells lies about how the product is made

c)      Gives accurate information about the product itself
d)      Mislead consumers as to where the goods are stored

33.   Market overt protects a buyer from any prosecution for the buying of
      encumbrance goods providing;
      a)      the goods are bought on a market day
      b)      the goods are bought during the market official opening times
      c)      the goods are bought when the market stalls are set up
              regardless of the time
      d)      the goods are bought from a market dealer.

34.   The Consumer Protection Act was enacted in
      a)      1997
      b)      2008
      c)      2007
      d)      1999

35.   The Sale of Goods and Supply of Services Act 1980 is a:
      a) prospective act
      b) retrospective act
      c) perspective act
      d) nominal act.

36.   Under the Sale of Goods and Supply of Services Act 1980 the term
      implied into the contract that the supplier will carry out the service
      with reasonable case and skills is treated as a:
      a)      Condition.
      b)      Warranty.
      c)      Innominate term.
      d)      Representation

37.   Susie bought a bike from "Best Bikes Ltd" telling the sales assistant
      that she knew nothing about bikes but wanted a bike suitable for
      riding on rough terrain. She bought the bike which was recommended
      to her by the assistant, however, although the bike was fine around
      town, the wheels and frame bent the first time she used it on rough
      terrain. Her action against "Best Bikes Ltd" would be for breach of
      which section of the Sale of Goods Act 1980?
      a)      12
      b)      13
      c)      14
      d)      15

38.   When do goods not have to be of a reasonable standard according to
      **S.14 of the SGSSA 1980**?
      a)      Second hand goods

b) Goods on sale
c) Issues brought to the attention of the buyer before the sale
d) They goods a bought online

39. A contract for the sale of goods is one where:
a) A seller gives goods to another by way of a contract, for safe keeping
b) Goods are passed to another to use in his business
c) A seller transfers or agrees to transfer, the property in goods to the buyer for a money consideration called the price
d) Goods are loaned under a contract of hire to a customer

40. What type of goods are not covered under the **Sale of Goods and Supply of Services Act 1980**
a) Cars
b) Automobiles
c) Crops from land for sale
d) Land

41. Where the transfer of the goods is to take place at a future time, this contract is called:
a) sale
b) an agreement to sell.
c) provisional sale
d) conditional sale

42. In a sales contract, a breach of a <u>condition</u> gives the aggrieved party right to:
a) repudiate the contract
b) claim damages
c) repudiate the contract and also claim damages
d) none of the above

43. In a sales contract, a breach of a <u>warranty</u> gives the aggrieved party right to:
a) repudiate the contract
b) claim damages
c) repudiate the contract and also claim damages
d) none of the above

44. The maxim is *"nemo det quod non habet"* which means that:
a) no one is an owner unless he pays for the goods
b) no one can give what he has not got
c) the sale of goods must be in writing

d)   none of the above

45.   A contract of sale of goods is a contract whereby the seller transfers or agrees to transfer the property:
a)   agreement to sell for a price
b)   an agreement to swap
c)   in goods to the buyer for a price
d)   none of the above

46.   A contract of sale of goods may be made:
a)   in writing
b)   orally,
c)   may be implied from the conduct of the parties.
d)   all of the above

47.   In a contract for sale of goods, they buyer may have an action, in respect of physical injuries caused by defect in the goods;
a)   against the manufacturer
b)   against the seller
c)   against the seller and also the manufacturer
d)   all of the above

48.   For the purpose of consumer law, which act defines a consumer;
a) The Consumer Protection Act 2007
b) Safety, health and Welfare at Work Act, 2005
c) The Sale of Goods Act 1983
d) The Sale of Goods and Supply of Services Act 1980

49.   A Condition is a stipulation which is:
a) important
b) unimportant
c) goes to the heart of the contract
d) gives the parties the power to choose importance

50.   A contract for the sale of goods includes
a) sale only
b) agreement to sell only
c) sale and agreement to sell
d) all of the above

## Section 5 – LO5 – Negotiable Instruments

### Negotiable Instruments

A negotiable *('transferable by delivery,')* instrument (*'a written document by which a right is created in favour of some person.'*) guarantees the payment of a specific amount of money, either on demand, or at a set time, with the payer named on the document.

(Explanation: NI literally means *'a written document which creates a right in favour of somebody and is freely transferable by delivery.'*) Examples of negotiable instruments include promissory notes, bills of exchange, banknotes, demand draft and cheques. Negotiable Instruments plays a major role in trading both nationally and internationally. "The term negotiable instrument does not have a statutory definition. To define the term the concept of 'instrument' and 'negotiability' requires a separate consideration, therefore any definition will be drawn from the common law." However, negotiable instruments are covered by **the Bill of Exchange Act 1882**, this act confers rights and privileges to the holder of the instrument and is described as a "title of money" and obliges the payment to the entitled possessor after completion and delivery of the contractual terms. Negotiable Instruments are mainly used to allow payment for exports and imports of trade Worldwide. Negotiable Instruments are not a common commodity in modern times with the advent of the computer and instant banking and transfers; however, they remain an important aspect of international trade

### Assignment

An assignment is the immediate transfer of existing property/proprietary rights, vested (already owned) or contingent (depending on a specific event), from the assignor to the assignee

### Chose in Action

An action to bring case for intangible goods (cannot be seen or touched) such as knowledge, patent, copyright etc. A share can also be intangible, as can stocks; however a savings bond cannot as it is non-transferable. These rights can only be enforced by action (bringing a legal case) and no actually physical possession is taken.

These rights can be legal or equitable. These rights include rights to:
- Shares
- Money due (debt)

- Rights/benefits under a contract
- Mortgagor's equity of redemption
- Beneficiary's rights and interests under a trust

**However, a stock or bond has a person's name and is NON transferable, there <u>NOT</u> a chose in action**

Types of Negotiable instrument

## *Promissory Note*

This is a negotiable instrument in writing with an unconditional undertaking/promise, signed by a maker, to pay a certain amount of money to the order, or bearer of the instrument.

A Promissory Note has the following characteristics
- It should be in writing
- It is an unconditional undertaking / promise to pay
- It should be signed by the maker / issuer.

There are only **two parties** to a promissory note –
1. the maker and;
2. the payee.
- Payable to both bearer and order of the instrument

## *Bills of Exchange*

A bill of exchange is a negotiable instrument in writing with an unconditional order, signed by a maker, ordering a certain person/institution, to pay a certain amount of money to the order, or bearer of the instrument.

A bill of exchange has the following characteristics
- It should be in writing
- It is an unconditional order to pay (not an undertaking) [refer previous post for the difference]
- It should be signed by the maker / issuer.

A bill of exchange has **three parties** –
1. the maker/drawer/issuer,
2. the drawee (may be a bank, or institution, or other person, whom the drawer is directing for payment to the payee) and
3. the payee (whom the drawer is paying)
- Payable to both bearer and order of the instrument

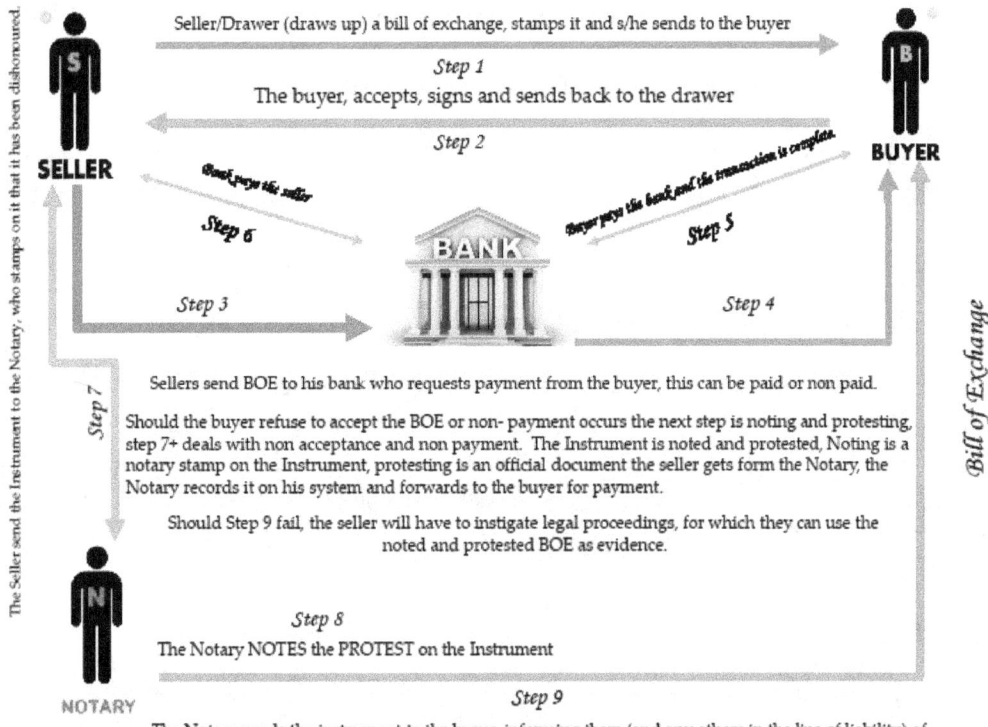

Step 10, after the formality of protesting and noting is finalised the holder can bring a civil case against _ALL_ of the parties to the bill in order to recover the amount due on the instrument.

## Cheques

A cheque is a distinct type of negotiable instrument, which is drawn on a specified banker (i.e., drawee is always a banker), and not expressed to be payable otherwise than on demand.

A Cheque has the following characteristics

* It is a special type of a negotiable instrument, where drawee is fixed (i.e., the banker)
* As it a Bill of Exchange, it is therefore an unconditional order to pay
* It should be signed by the maker / issuer (i.e., the account holder of a bank).

A cheque has **three parties** -
1. the drawer (e.g. account holder),
2. the drawee (always banker), and
3. the payee (whom the drawer is paying)

- It should be paid on demand (i.e., whenever the cheque is presented to the bank)
- Payable to both bearer and order of the instrument

Example - The drawer is the individual who issues the cheque, instructing the bank (drawee) to pay the recipient (payee)

## Crossing cheques

Crossing is an extra protection, there are three parties to a cheque the payer, the bank and the payee, and if it is crossed it must go through the payees account. *"An uncrossed cheque could be written by A to B, endorsed by B and given to C, if C presents it and it is rejected, C can sue either B or A, leaving A in a vulnerable position as they were not party to the transaction between B and C"*

### *Making changes to a cheque*

Changes can be made and signed (initialled) by the payer, i.e. a stale cheque (out of date, can be redated) however, most banks may reject this as suspicious. Cheques crossed with **"& Co" or "Not Negotiable**" – should be lodged into AN account (does not have to specified, who). Cheques crossed with **"Account Payee Only"** -requires that the cheque should be lodged to an account *IN THE NAME* of the payee

Cheques crossed with "**Account payee only - XXX Bank, YYYY Branch** - requires that the cheque be lodged to an account in the **name of the payee** in the **specified Branch**

### *Types of endorsements for negotiable or other instruments*

### *Holder for value*

This occurs when there is a defective title, which the holder was given notice of.

### *Holder in due course*

The holder has obtained the bill in good faith for valuable consideration without notice, however it turns out the original holder had bad title (no right to have it/issue it), the holder keeps good title.

### *Arab Bank V Ross*

Where there was an error on the face of a promissory note as the word 'Company' did not appear, therefore giving the impression of forgery.

### LO5 – MCQ's

1. How many parties are there to a "Promissory note" and a "bill of exchange"?
   a) There are three parties to a "Promissory note" and three to a "bill of exchange"
   b) There are five parties to a "Promissory note" and two to a "bill of exchange
   c) There is one party to a "Promissory note" and three to a "bill of exchange"
   d) There are two parties to a "Promissory note and three to a bill of exchange"

2. Where a cheque has been issued, and there is a discrepiency between the amount in words and figures, which shall be paid
   a) the amount in figures
   b) the amount written in words
   c) the cheque is void
   d) none of the above.

3. 'Negotiable' means transferable. In the case of a negotiable instrument Negotiation can take place from one person to another:
   a) by mere delivery or by endorsement and delivery.
   b) only by endorsement and delivery to the drawee
   c) delivery is not negotiation
   d) none of the above

4. Money orders; Postal orders and Share certificates; are examples of:
   a) Negotiable Instruments
   b) Non-negotiable instruments
   c) A mix of Negotiable and Non- Negotiable Instruments
   d) None of the above

5. A bill of exchange, when it is not payable on demand, is entitled to get:
   a) 3 days grace period.
   b) 10 days grace period
   c) the day of maturity only
   d) none of the above

6. Where a negotiable instrument is dishonoured, notice is given to:
   a) drawer only
   b) all previous endorsees.
   c) drawer and all previous endorsees.

    d)   none of the above

7. The undertaking contained in a promissory note, to pay a certain sum of money is
   a) conditional
   b) unconditional
   c) may be conditional or unconditional depending upon the circumstances
   d) none of the above.

8. A bill of exchange contains a/an
   a) unconditional undertaking
   b) unconditional order
   c) conditional undertaking
   d) conditional order.

9. A Cheque is a
   a) promissory note
   b) bill of exchange
   c) both (a) and (b) above
   d) None of the above.

10. A promissory note or bill of exchange which is not expressed to be payable on demand, at sight or on presentment is at maturity
    a) on the 30th day after the day on which it is expressed to be payable
    b) on the 3rd day after the day on which it is expressed to be payable
    c) on the 5th day after the day on which it is expressed to be payable
    d) on the 4th day after the day on which it is expressed to be payable.

11. In a promissory note, the amount of money payable
    a) must be certain
    b) may be certain or uncertain
    c) is usually uncertain
    d) none of the above.

12. A bill is drawn payable to 'A' or order. 'A' indorses it to 'B', the indorsement not containing the words '"or order" or any equivalent words. Can 'B' negotiate the instrument?
    a) yes
    b) no
    c) not always
    d) none of the above

13. The endorsement of a negotiable instrument followed by delivery
    a) transfers to the endorsee the property in the bill, provided the endorsement must be an endorsement in full
    b) does not transfer the property in the bill to anyone
    c) transfers to the endorsee the property in the bill
    d) transfers to the holder the property in bill.

14. If the words "not negotiable" are used with special crossing in a cheque, the cheque is
    a) not transferable
    b) transferable
    c) negotiable under certain circumstances
    d) none of the above.

15. Crossing of a cheque effects the
    a) negotiability of the cheque
    b) mode of payment on the cheque
    c) both (a) and (b)
    d) none of the above.

16. Dishonour by non-acceptance takes place
    a) when the bill is properly presented for acceptance, except where presentment is excused, but the drawee makes the default in accepting it
    b) when the Bill is properly presented for acceptance, except where presentment is excused, but the drawee makes the default in paying it
    c) when the bill is properly presented for payment, except where presentment is excused, but the drawee fails to accept it
    d) none of the above.

17. When a cheque has become invalid because of the expiry of the stipulated period, can it be re-validated by the drawer by alteration of dates?
    a) yes, the drawer can re-validate the cheque by alteration of dates
    b) no, the drawer cannot re-validate it by so alteration of dates
    c) although the drawer cannot revalidate the cheque, but the drawee can at his discretion reissue it
    d) none of the above.

18. A protest must contain
    a) the name of the person for whom the instrument has been protested
    b) the name of the person against whom the instrument has been protested

    c) the instrument itself or its literal transcript
    d) all of the above.

19. A protest is made by
    a) the drawer
    b) the endorser
    c) a notary
    d) none of the above.

20. Where a cheque is crossed generally the banker on whom it is drawn
    a) shall not pay it otherwise than to a banker
    b) shall not pay it otherwise than to the holder
    c) shall not pay it to a banker
    d) none of the above.

## Section 6 – LO6 – Business Organisations - Company law

### Partnerships

***Section 1(2) of the Partnership Act 1890***, states that a partnership is a "relationship which subsists between persons carrying on a business in common with a view to profit."

### Partnership agreement
Main clauses
   a) Names of Partners
   b) Address of the Business
   c) Business of the Partnership
   d) Partnership property
   e) Loans to the Partnership
   f) Banking arrangements
   g) Records and accounts
   h) Meetings and voting
   i) Restrictions on Partners
   j) Expulsion
   k) Termination of the Partnership
   l) Indemnity for the Partnership

### Types of partnership

**General** (must have at least one general partner) = sleeping (can have no involvement in the business, usually investor, with no skill, but has money to invest)
**Limited Partner** (Register with the CRO. Liability is limited to the capital investment, cannot be involved the day to day running of the business).

A partnership is the coming together of two or more persons and in return for the benefits received, such as extra capital and expertise from the others engaged jointly in the venture. Partnerships in contrast, are not legal entities: there may be a name attached to the firm but the partnership consists solely of the individual partners and the firm has no independent legal existence.

## Number of partners

Maximum number of partners in a **general partnership** = 20, **banking and financial institutions is** = 10
It must be noted that where the partnership is **commercial or industrial** the maximum number of partners is 50,
***S1435 c) iv) 1 of the Companies Act 2014***

## Liability of partners

The partners share the profits of their venture, the assets and liabilities, liable for the actions of all other partners, jointly a severely liable.

## Dissolution of partnerships

Dissolution of a partnership can occur by
1. Automatically e.g. on the death or bankruptcy of a partner
2. By notice, any partner can just dissolve the partnership by giving notice in the absence of any express or implied contrary agreement.
3. illegality-partnerships formed to carry out an illegal activity or an activity contrary to public policy are automatically dissolved
4. By expiration-either at the end of the partnership term or on the completion of a specific undertaking for which the partnership was formed
5. Dissolution by the Court

Court Dissolution where:
- a partner is of unsound mind
- a partner becomes permanently incapable of performing his part of the partnership contract
- a partner's behaviour is prejudicially affecting the partnership business
- a partner is in breach of the partnership agreement
- where the partnership can only be carried on at a loss
- Where it is just and equitable to dissolve the partnership.

## Types of company

### Private Company Limited by Shares (LTD)

The LTD is a private company limited by shares formed for a lawful purpose where the liability of the shareholder/member is limited to the amount, if any, unpaid on the shares registered in their name at that time.

Key features
* No requirement for the LTD to have an authorised share capital.
* A LTD will be able to dispense with holding a physical AGM, irrespective of the number of shareholders.
* Can have between 1 and 149 shareholders;
* Can have 1 or more directors;
* Must have a company secretary;
* Must have a one-document constitution;
* Name must end in "Limited" or "Ltd";
* Cannot have an objects clause because it has full unlimited capacity
* The board (including a sole director), and any person registered with the CRO as having authority, will be deemed to have authority to bind the company.

### The Designated Activity Company (DAC)

A DAC has the status of a private company and can be formed for any lawful purpose by any person or persons subscribing to a constitution and complying with relevant sections of the Companies Act.

### The format of a DAC can be either:
a)    a private company limited by shares, or
b)    a private company limited by guarantee and having a share capital.

Key features
* Constitution is in the form of a memorandum and articles of association and contains an objects clause detailing its permitted activities;
* Can list any debt securities for offer to the public, unlike the LTD;
* Company name must end with "designated activity company" or DAC;
* Can have between 1 and 149 shareholders;
* Must have at least two directors and where there is more than one member it cannot dispense with AGM's.

## The Public Limited Company (PLC) Key features

A public limited company (PLC) is a company limited by shares and having a share capital which is not less than the authorised minimum of €25,000. A PLC's constitution is in the form of a memorandum and articles of association and contains an objects clause. It has the capacity to offer, allot and issue securities to the public.

* The format of a Public Limited Company (PLC) can be either:
  a) an investment company with its sole objects of collective investment of funds, or
  b) a public company other than an investment company;
* The main feature of a PLC is that it can establish with a minimum of one member and no maximum limit. It must have a minimum of two directors and the directors have a duty to ensure that the person appointed as company secretary has the skill necessary to carry out his/her statutory duty. A PLC is required to hold an AGM and have its financial statements audited and a traded company is required to include a
  "corporate governance statement" in its director's report;

## Private Unlimited Company (ULC)

A ULC is a private unlimited company with a share capital formed for any lawful purpose by the subscribers to the constitution and complying with relevant sections of the Companies Act. Unlimited companies are not generally used as trading companies as the liability of the members is not limited and in a winding up situation the members are obliged to pay all the debts of the company.

Some of the features of a ULC are that it may be formed with just one member, it must have a minimum of two directors, it must hold AGMs, and it is not required to attach financial statements to its annual return.

### *Guarantee Companies*

A Company Limited by Guarantee or "CLG" is a company which does not have a share capital and where the member's liability is limited by its constitution to such amount the members undertake to contribute to the assets of the company in the event of it being wound up. A CLG is required to have a minimum of 2 directors, it is required to hold

AGM's and a CLG that is not a credit institution or an insurance undertaking may avail of audit exemption if they satisfy the conditions specified.

## Key features

- Cannot have a share capital;
- Can have just one member, and no maximum number of members;
- Can have an objects clause (although the Act seeks to oust the operation of the doctrine of ultra vires by providing that the validity of an act done by a DAC shall not be questioned on the ground of lack of capacity);
- Its name must end with "company limited by guarantee" (or "CLG", "C.L.G", "clg" or "c.l.g.") or the Irish equivalent, save where application made to dispense with this requirement;
- Is not prevented from having its debentures admitted to trading or listed;
- Must have at least two directors;
- Unless constitution provides otherwise: directors shall retire by rotation;
  o directors' remuneration (if any) must be determined by the members in general meeting;
- CLG may not dispense with holding an AGM where it has more than one member;
- Key feature is that it does not have requirements in relation to the form of the
  o share capital i.e. it has members, not shareholders;
- Likely to be the legal form of choice for the many charities, sports and social clubs and management companies which are currently incorporated as public companies limited by guarantee without a share capital.

**Limited by Shares** = a company whose members are liable upon liquidation for any unpaid share capital which they have not paid.

**Limited by guarantee** = (usually non-profits or charities) a company whose members guarantee to pay a set amount of money should the company go into liquidation, there is no shares and no issued capital.

| Private company limited by shares (LTD) | Designated activity company (DAC) |
|---|---|
| <ul><li>This has a single-document called the constitution,</li><li>Unlimited capacity to trade (any kind of business as there is no objects clause,)</li><li>The board (or person registered as a board) may bind the company,</li></ul> | <ul><li>Very similar to an existing private company,</li><li>The have an objects clause,</li><li>The directors can act ultra vires, this does not invalidate transactions with third parties, Remedies for members/liability for directors if acting beyond</li></ul> |

| | |
|---|---|
| • Requires only have one director (it must have a different secretary) and one member,<br>• May avoid holding AGM with a written resolution, and<br>• May not offer securities (shares, debt, and so on) to the public or list securities.<br>• | capacity,<br>• Limited by shares,<br>• Minimum two directors,<br>• May avoid holding AGM only if a single member company, and<br>• May list certain debentures. |
| **Company limited by guarantee (CLG), public limited company (PLC), and unlimited company (UC)**<br>• The minimum number of members is one,<br>• Objects clause and ultra vires – see DAC,<br>• Existing law largely restated (but see subsequent articles in this series), and<br>• CLG may avail of audit exemption. | **Names**<br>An LTD must have 'Limited' or 'Ltd' as part of its name. All companies must use their abbreviation<br><br>**Share capital requirements**<br><br>**Ltd** = no minimum share capital **no authorised share capital requirements**<br>**DAC** = no minimum share minimum of 25% of issued share capital must be paid<br>**PLC** = €25,000 issued share capital. |

**Shareholders Rights**

*Right to Information*

Shareholders have the right to inspect and obtain copies of information and documentation pertaining to the company, including the company registers, minutes of general meetings, memorandum and articles of association, financial statements, and auditors' reports.

*Right to Attend & Vote at Meetings*

Each shareholder has the right to receive notice of general meetings of the company, to attend at those meetings and to vote on issues raised.

*Right to Dividends*

Dividends are payments made to shareholders out of a company's distributable profits. Shareholders do not have an automatic right to receive dividend payments and there is no legal obligation on a company to declare a dividend, even in circumstances where it is in funds to do so.

## Rights on the Winding up Of A Company

### *Legal Proceedings*

A shareholder has a right to commence legal proceedings against the company where the affairs of the company are being conducted in a manner oppressive to any shareholder, or in disregard of any shareholders' interests. Conduct is oppressive when it is burdensome, harsh and wrongful.

## Directors / Directors duties

**Directors**, "any person occupying the position of director by whatever name called".

### Types of Directors

**Executive** (an executive director will also be an employee of the company, they run the company as a whole)

**Non-executive** = is not employed by the company, people from outside the company who have a special expertise or experience, self-employed)

**De facto** = is a person who has not been formally appointed but who in effect acts as if he were a director).

**Shadow directors** = overseers of the board, the directors normally act in according to the instruction of the shadow).

**Managing director** = this is the manager with the responsibilities of the day to day running of the company, they have the veto vote at meeting and also known as the CEO)

## Director's duties

Section 228 the Companies Act 2014 sets out the following 8 duties of directors, 6 of which are derived from common law and 2 of which were previously included in company law:

1. To act in good faith in what the director considers to be the interests of the company;
2. To act honestly and responsibly in relation to the conduct of the affairs of the company (this duty was previously set out in law under section 150 of the Companies Act 1990);
3. To act in accordance with the company's constitution and exercise his or her powers only for the purposes allowed by law;
4. Not to use the company's property, information or opportunities for his or her own or anyone else's benefit (unless in specific allowed circumstances);

5. Not to agree to a restriction of his/her exercise of independent judgement (unless in specific allowed circumstances);
6. To avoid any conflict of interest between the director's duties to the company and his/her own interests (unless in specified allowed circumstances);
7. To exercise the care, skill and diligence which would be exercised in the same circumstances by a reasonable person;
8. To have regard to the interests of the members of the company, in addition to the duty under section 224 to have regard to the interests of the company's employees in general (this duty was previously set out in law under section 52 of the Companies Act 1990).

**Also:**

**Duly to appoint a company secretary** with the skills necessary to discharge his/her statutory duties, Duty to prepare and deliver a 'Section 19' constitution, Duty to prepare a directors' compliance statement.

**Appointment and removal of directors** = **appointment;** the first directors are appointed by the formators and then by the re-elected by the board and members) **removal,** = by ordinary resolution at a general meeting. (fair procedures **must** be followed as they are employees)

## Company finance

**Crystallisation of floating charges**, this occurs when the company is put into liquidation (only in liquidation, not receivership), the floating charges such as stock or book debt now becomes solid and only the liquidator can sell it, it cannot be exchanged for invoices or cash in fact even if it is your own charge the liquidator must sell all charges and pay everyone in the priority of charges,

**Fixed charge**, this is a debenture (company loan) taken out against fixed solid objects such as property buildings etc., they are repayable in the order they were registered.

**Floating charge**, this is a charge taken out when a company may not have much in the way of solid buildings etc., they may work in a services industry and only have book debt (accountant etc.), therefore the banks (debenture holder) can take a debenture on their "book debt", this is lower in priority to fixed charges but also payable in order of registration.

## Registration of charges

Failure to register particulars of a registerable charge within 21 days after the date of its "creation" will render the charge void against any creditor or liquidator of the company.

## Share Capital

This means the amount of capital raised by the issue of shares, by a company. The shareholders are the owners of the company. The total share capital is divided into small parts and each part is called a share. A share is the smallest part of the total capital of a company.

## Company Capital

### *Authorised capital*

The maximum amount of capital the company intends to raise/issue or the company can legally raise/issue from shareholders, i.e. many companies state in their constitution that they will have 1,000,000 shares at €1, this is their authorised share capital. (*They cannot sell more shares than this or obtain loans for any more*) If they wish to raise more than this they need to pass a special resolution to change the authorised share capital in the constitutional documents.

### Issued capital

This is how many shares have been released by the company, i.e. the company may have sold 100,000 shares @ €1 each, therefore their issued capital is 100,000 share = €100,000 euro.

### Called up capital

This is the amount which the company have received from their issued shares, i.e. shareholders do not have to pay the full amount on shares when they purchase, they only have to pay a minimum of 25%, so although there may be issued capital of €100,000 there may only be €25,000 called up (*or paid up*)

### Reserve capital

This is the amount which is left to be paid on the party paid share (*above*) which the shareholder is liable to pay should the company go into liquidation.

### Audit/Auditors

### Exempt from audit

**H**aving a turnover of no more than €8.8m; having no more than €4.4 million as its balance sheet total; having no more than 50 employees, on average; and being up to date with its filing obligations with the Registrar of Companies.

### Appoint an Auditor

The directors of a new company appoint the first auditor. Subsequently, the company's members appoint or reappoint the auditor at each annual general meeting (AGM).

### Duties of an Auditor

**Duty to provide a report** (their opinion the company's financial statements give a true and fair view).

**Duty to report failure to maintain proper books of account** (i*f the auditors form this opinion they must notify the company that they have not kept proper books of account*) they must inform the CRO after 7 days if the company does not get the books in order. **Duty to report indictable offences** (*an indictable offence is an offence that is serious and will be tried before a judge and jury in the Circuit Court*).

**Duty to explain reasons for resigning** ( *they must state if they **HAVE** a reason to believe there is anything to be brought to the attention of shareholder or they **DO NOT** believe there is anything to be brought to the attention of the shareholders*).

**Duty to exercise professional integrity** (*they must carry out an audit with professional integrity*), they have a **duty to exercise reasonable skill and care**; they may be liable for damages to the company if they don't.

## Rights of auditors

Auditors have the right to: **access the books** and accounts of the company and its subsidiaries; **access information and explanations** from the company's directors and employees; **be notified** of company general meetings and attend and address the meetings; and **explain** at a general meeting the circumstances of any proposal to remove them as auditor and to contest that removal.

## Company Meetings

### AGM

Annual general meeting, part of the financial calendar, the board present the year's results, discuss the outlook for the coming year, present the audited accounts and to have the final dividend and directors' pay approved by shareholders. Shareholder vote on and pass **resolutions**, voting is done on either a **show of hands** (*one vote per member*) or **poll** (*one vote per share, therefore the more shares the more say*) in which shareholders vote in proportion to their holdings.

### EGM

Issues need to be addressed and approved that cannot wait until the next AGM, such as constitutional changes or where a company having a share capital, such number of members who hold, not less than one-tenth of such of the paid-up share capital of the company.

**AR = Annual Return**; this is the return sent to the CRO.
**ARD = Annual Return Date**, this is the date for which the company must for its existence (*lifetime*) submit its returns to the CRO, the ARD is six (6) months from the date of "incorporation (***not application nor receipt***), therefore the first ARD is 6 months + the 12 months, making it 18 months form the Incorporation date.

## Resolutions

A resolution is written document describing an action that has been authorised by either the directors or members of a company (*written agreement*).
**Ordinary resolution, 50%+** is for normal day to day, plus removal of directors etc.

**Special resolution 75+** change in structure, change in name, change in authorised share capital (a change in this could dilute shares so needs 75% majority)

## Company Conclusion

## Examinership

Examinership is a process whereby a company seeks the protection of the High Court while negotiating a structured settlement with creditors. The company is protected from any form of action, they have 4 months to get the agreement and structured, the examiner decided on a plan of action. The company continues to run, the directors remain in place.

## Receivership

The company cannot pay its debts and a receiver is sent into help the company to realise and pay debtors, the directors duties are set aside (until all debt paid) there is priority of payment, when the debts are paid the company directors can come back and run the company, the debenture holder can remove the receiver at any time.

## Liquidation

A company is considered to be insolvent under Irish law if it is unable to pay its debts.

## Creditors Voluntary Liquidation

An insolvent company voluntarily decides to go into liquidation, (they are not brought into the court process), this is usually initiated by the company's directors, they hold a board meeting to agree that the company should be placed into administration, notices should be sent to shareholders and creditors, ten days' notice of the meeting must be given to all creditors, this meeting must be advertised at least ten days before the meeting in at least two daily newspapers which circulate in the district where the registered office or the main place of business of the company is situated, the director/s are also required to present a Statement of Affairs which describes the book value of the company's assets together with their realisable value.

## Members Voluntary Liquidation

This occurs when a directors decide to retire, or when a company has run its course, to realise its assets and distribute its surplus to the shareholders, it is initiated by the shareholders and there is no creditor involvement. A Declaration of Solvency must be signed by the directors stating that the company can pay any remaining debts in full within 12 months. The company is dissolved following completion of the liquidation.

## Compulsory Liquidation

This occurs because of a winding up order on the order of a court from a petition of a creditor, the Director of Corporate enforcement, A shareholder, or the company itself. An Official Liquidator is appointed by the Court with powers to liquidate a company, investigate its activities and pursue directors.

## The ODCE

**Improving Public Understanding of Company Law Rights and Duties**
Raising Standards of Compliance
Deepening our Relationship with Stakeholders
Influencing Policy Development
**Confronting Unlawful Company Law Behaviour**
Identifying Suspected Misconduct
Enforcing Serious Breaches under the Companies Acts
**Providing Quality Services to Internal and External Customers**
Securing and Prudently Managing our Resources
Developing Staff
Improving our Customer Services

## Memorandum of Association

The memorandum of association is the main document by which the registration of a company is achieved and the provisions contained within the memorandum will prevail over any conflicting provisions contained in the articles of association. The memorandum of association has five compulsory clauses:
- The name clause;

- The object's clause;
- The liability clause;
- The capital clause; and
- The subscription clause

## Objects clause

An **objects clause** is a provision in a company's constitution stating the purpose and range of activities for which the company is carried on

## The Articles of Association

The Articles of Association govern the internal management of the company, it literally lays down how a company is to be governed normally by choosing a standard set of Articles provided within the Companies Acts' with appropriate amendments.

The objects are clauses stated in your company's memorandum of association stating the principal activity of the business and the subsidiary activities.

## Constitution / Articles of Association / memorandum of Association

## Company formation / registration

The incorporation and registration of a company commences with the delivery of The Articles of Association / memorandum of Association /Constitution, with the Form A1, together with a statement of consent and declaration in accordance with the Companies Act to the Registrar of Companies. On the registration of the constitution, the Registrar will certify in writing that the company is incorporated and issue a certificate of incorporation.

## The CRO

The CRO has a number of core functions:
- The incorporation of companies and the registration of business names.
- The receipt and registration of post incorporation documents.
- The enforcement of the Companies Act 2014 in relation to the filing obligations of companies.
- Making information available to the public.

**Section 6 MCQ's**

1.    Sources of company law
      a) Company law Legislation,
      b) Case law and Precedent
      c) EU law
      d) Code of Ethics

2.    A Public company can
      a) Sell shares on stock market,
      b) Can't sell shares on the open market
      c) Transfer shares by deed
      d) Swap shares

3.    A Private company
      a) Can't sell shares to public (only transfer),
      b) Can sell shares to the public
      c) Sell shares at their annual general meeting
      d) None of the above

4.    When a company is Limited by shares it's
      a) Shareholders' liability is limited to their investments
      b) Shareholders are liable for all losses
      c) Shareholders are liable for all losses which they were aware the
         company were making
      d) Shareholders are jointly and liable for losses which stem from their
         involvement in the decisions

5.    The Doctrine of a Separate legal personality
      a) A company is a legal person separate and distinct from its
         members - can enter contracts, be sued, own assets
      b) A company is a NOT legal person separate and distinct from its
         members.  The directors own the company
      c) A company is not liable for contracts its directors enter on their
         behalf

6.    The Doctrine of Ultra Vires occurs
      a) When a company enters contracts which they have the power to do
      b) When a company enters a contract which they do not have the
         power to do
      c) When a director employs a shadow director
      d) When the shareholders agree on directs remuneration

7. The Director Manages the Company on behalf of shareholders
   a) True
   b) False

8. Which is the most common type of registered company?
   a) An unlimited company
   b) A company limited by guarantee
   c) A private company limited by shares
   d) A public limited company

9. A sole trader's liability for debts incurred in the course of business is limited to the value of business assets.
   a) True
   b) False

10. Which of the following is not a type of capital?
    a) Allotted capital
    b) Paid up capital
    c) Debenture capital
    d) Issued capital

11. Which of the following does not describe the nature of a floating charge?
    a) It is a charge over a class of assets both present and future book debts
    b) It is a charge over a class of asset which, in the ordinary course of business, changes from time to time
    c) It is a charge that requires the company to obtain consent if it wishes to deal with the charged asset in the ordinary course of business.
    d) It is a charge over stock in trade, raw material and finished articles

12. Which of the following statements describes the decision of the House of Lords in *Salomon v Salomon & Co Ltd (1897)?*
    a) A company has unlimited liability for its debts
    b) A company cannot issue floating charges to its members
    c) A company is a legal entity, distinct from its members
    d) A single member cannot form a company

13. Which of the following statements is not a correct proposition in relation to the role of a promoter of a company?
    a) A person who takes the necessary steps to form a company
    b) A person who owes fiduciary duties to a company
    c) A person who is acts as a director of a company during the course of the promotion of the company

d) A person who can become a member of a company on incorporation of the company

14. Which body exercises the control of a registered company?
    a) The general meeting
    b) The board of directors
    c) The company secretary
    d) The general meeting and the board of directors

15. Which of the following describes a director with day to day responsibility for a company and its board of directors?
    a) Chairman
    b) Finance Director
    c) President
    d) Managing director

16. Which of the following is not a true statement relating to the nature and scope of fraudulent trading as contained in Companies Act 2014?
    a) In the course of the winding up, it appears that any business of the company has been carried on with intent to defraud creditors of the company or for any fraudulent purpose.
    b) The liquidator can apply to the court for a declaration that any persons who were knowingly parties to the carrying on of the business in this way be liable to make such contributions to the company's assets as the court thinks proper.
    c) Fraudulent trading means conduct that is Knowingly and intentionally dishonest according to the notions of ordinary decent business people.
    d) Only directors or officers of the company can have action taken against them

17. The Minimum number of members in case of private company is
    a) 1
    b) 2
    c) 3
    d) 4

18. Liability of a member in case of a private company is
    a) Limited
    b) Unlimited
    c) Both (a) or (b)
    d) None of the above

19. Maximum no. of persons in case of partnership banking business
_____
   a) 10
   b) 20
   c) 30
   d) 5

20. Minimum paid up share capital in case of a DAC is _____
   a) 10%
   b) 100%
   c) 25%
   d) 50%

21. Minimum no. of Directors in case of a LTD is _____
   a) 1
   b) 2
   c) 3
   d) 4

22. Minimum no. of Directors in case of DAC is _____
   a) 1
   b) 2
   c) 3
   d) 4

23. Transfer of shares in the partnership firm is
   a) Restricted
   b) Freely transferable
   c) Prohibited
   d) None of the above

24. Generally Company liability is
   a) Limited
   b) Unlimited
   c) Unlimited by shares
   d) None of the above

25. The companies which are formed under special Act. Those companies are known as
   a) Chartered companies
   b) Statutory companies
   c) Registered companies
   d) None of these

26. The companies which are formed under Companies Act. 2014. They will be known as
    a) Chartered companies
    b) Statutory companies
    c) Registered companies
    d) None of these

27. Transfer of shares in the case of public company is
    a) Prohibited
    b) Restricted
    c) Freely transferable
    d) None of these

28. Private company can start its business immediately after the issue of

    a) Certificate of commencement
    b) Certificate of Incorporation
    c) Both of the above
    d) None of the above

29. Public company should start business only after getting certificate of
    a) Incorporation
    b) Trading Certificate
    c) Commencement certificate
    d) All of the above

30. A company can change its name at its own discretion by passing
    _____
    a) Ordinary resolution
    b) Special resolution
    c) Boards resolution
    d) None of the above

### Section 7 – LO7

**Corporate governance**

This is how a company is run; self-governance and legislative requirements.

Sources of Corporate governance;

**Combined code**; **L.A.R.R.E**, *Leadership, Accountability, Remuneration, Relationships with shareholders, Effectiveness* –
**Company law**; *the Companies Act 2014* –
**Criminal law**; *Corporate Law Enforcement Act 2001; Criminal Justice (theft and fraud related offences) Act 2001, the Companies(auditing and accounting) Act 2003* –
**Common law;** (case law such as fiduciary duties);
**Constitutional documents;** a DACs or Plc.'s Constitutional documents;
**The Listing Rules**; the rules that cover companies who trade on the stock market.

**L.A.R.R.E**

The aim of the code is to provide a set if principals that ensure company directors take responsibility for their actions and provide sufficient disclosure at regular intervals on the financial status of their company. It contains the following principles: (Source- UK code of Corporate Governance)

**THE COMBINED CODE**

*Leadership:*

Every company should be headed by an effective board which is collectively responsible for company's long term success. The chairman is responsible for leadership of the board and ensuring its effectiveness on all aspects of its role.

*Accountability:*

The board should present a balanced and understandable assessment of the company's position and prospects.

### Relations with shareholders:

There should be a dialogue with shareholders based on the mutual understanding of objectives. The board has responsibility for ensuring that a satisfactory dialogue takes place with shareholders.

### Remuneration

Directors pay is transparent and how it is decided is transparent, they must not be paid more than they are worth but also must be enough to attract them and retain them, directors have no input or say in their pat

### Effectiveness

The board and its committees should have appropriate balance of skills, experience, independence and knowledge of the company to enable them to discharge their respective duties and responsibilities.
There should be a formal, rigorous and transparent procedure for the appointment of new directors to the board.

Company law offences

### Fraudulent trading

Where any person (anyone who is aware of the fraud, even down to floor staff) knowingly and intentionally sets out to defraud the creditors of a company. Liability; Liable for some or all of the company's debts in civil law and in criminal law (summary, up to 12 months, indictable; 10 years and up to €500,000 fine or both).

### Reckless trading

A company officer knowingly being part to the reckless running of a company, it must be proved that the officer didn't act as a reasonable officer of their skill and e3xperience would and cause a loss to the company, they recklessly carried on business knowing they could not pay their debts when they fell due. Liability; personally liable for the debts of the company.

### Money Laundering

Attempt to turn cash or proceeds of crime into genuine assets, the Elements: concealing or disguising; converting or transferring; removing from or bring into the state. Processes; Placement (into businesses etc.) Layering (move from business to business) Integrating (using as part of income and appears legit). Sanctions; summary – fine up to€5k or 12 months. Indictable – up to 14 years and fine.

### Insider dealing

When a party has access to or has price sensitive information regarding a company's performance, they then deal with those shares to make a profit, the insider dealer makes use of the sensitive information which is not known outside of the company, or they give (sell ) that information to a third party. An insider is anyone who uses their employment, contracts, shareholding or illegal activity to gain access to the information, insider information is; precise nature, not made public, relates to shares or securities, could impact the price if released, entice a person to buy as part of their portfolio. They cannot use, disclose or induce another with the information. The person obtaining the information and any third party who is aware it is sensitive face up to 10 years in prison and 10m in fines.

## Ethical Standards for Accountants in Ireland

The scandal caused by the collapse of Polly Peck (Asil Nadir) in 1993 with £1.3bn in debts in its wake, followed by the collapse of Enron in 2002 which brought down Arthur Anderson's (auditing) firm, only goes to show how important that there be an established set of rules concerning ethical behaviour. Recently the world has been surprised by the $2.5 Billion accounting fraud in India by Satyam Computer Services. Here in Ireland in 2010 saw the Anglo Irish Bank scandal, was involved financial report manipulation, which resulted in the Government having to pump in over €22 Billion Anglo Irish Bank, closely followed in 2012 by the uncovering of corruption at the frozen seafood giant Pescanova; who were accused of false billing and hiding debt of €3.3 billion.

Due to endlessly unethical behaviour of accounting fraud, the Unites States government have introduced the ***Sarbanes-Oxley Act (2002)*** in and tightened regulation in Ireland and European countries. The IFAC (*International Federation of Accountants Committee*) introduced new ethical standards which were designed to eliminate fraud in the accountancy profession.

## CPA ACCA ATI Code of Ethics

### Integrity (being honest, even when no one is watching)

Straightforward and honest in all professional and business relationships, fair
dealing and truthfulness.

### Objectivity

Do not to compromise the profession or business judgment because of bias, conflict of interest or the undue influence of others.

### Professional competence and due care

Maintain professional knowledge and skill and to act diligently, in accordance with applicable technical and professional.

### Confidentiality

Keep information confidential; take all reasonable steps to preserve confidentiality. Ensure all unpublished information about a client's or employer's affairs are confidential.

# CPA/ACCA/ATI - BUSINESS LAW CRAM NOTES

## *Professional behaviour*

Comply with relevant laws and regulations and avoid any action that may discredit or adversely affect the good reputation of the profession.

### Threats to the fundamental Principles

In order to do so, it is important to be alert to situations that may threaten these fundamental principles. Identified threats need to be evaluated and managed, to ensure that they are either eliminated or reduced to an acceptable level.

Threats may arise as a result of any of the following:
- self-interest: the threat that a financial or other interest will inappropriately influence your judgement or behaviour
- self-review: the threat that you will not properly evaluate the results of a previous judgement made or service performed by you (or someone else within the organisation) when forming a judgement as part of providing a current service
- advocacy: the threat that you will promote a position (usually your employer's) to the point that your objectivity is compromised
- familiarity: the threat that, due to a long or close relationship with someone, you will be too sympathetic to that person's interests, or too accepting of their work
- intimidation: the threat that you will be deterred from acting objectively because of actual or perceived pressures, including attempts to exercise undue influence over you.

When resolving an ethical conflict, consider carefully whether other parties could or should be involved in discussions and, if appropriate, how those parties should be approached. You should keep in mind confidentiality obligations. If you are facing, or think you might be facing, an ethical dilemma, you may wish to seek advice from a trusted colleague within the organisation, your professional body or an independent lawyer.

### Self-Review Threats (examples)

Examples of circumstances that create self-review threats for a professional accountant in public practice include:
- A firm issuing an assurance report on the effectiveness of the operation of financial systems after designing or implementing the systems.
- A firm having prepared the original data used to generate records that are the subject matter of the assurance engagement.

- A member of the assurance team being, or having recently been, a director or officer of the client.
- A member of the assurance team being, or having recently been, employed by the client in a position to exert significant influence over the subject matter of the engagement.
- The firm performing a service for an assurance client that directly affects the subject matter information of the assurance engagement.

| Ethical Standards (APB IFAC) | Code of Ethics; **The Five fundamental principles** |
|---|---|
| **1. Integrity, Objectivity and Independence**<br>*Be open and honest in all dealings, take every case and client at their face value, do not make judgements without the facts and be unbiased, and finally do not allow anyone to sway decision making, remain independent in decision making.*<br>**2. Financial, Business and Personal Relationships.**<br>*Do not hold a financial interest in any clients business, this is the same for family members., do not loan staff out to clients unless this member of staff is removed from that clients account, if a member of the clients business comes to work for you, you must ensure that all connections to the previous employment are severed.*<br>**3. Long Association with the Audit Engagement**<br>*Where a senior member of the audit team is in long association or has a long relationship with the client it is advisable that their association is checked and monitored to ensure that objectivity and independence is not threatened. For instance, familiarity, and decision may be made in haste or because of "friendship"*<br>**4. Fees, Remuneration, and evaluation, litigation, gifts and hospitality.**<br>*The firm must ensure that the fees are appropriate to the contract, not as to how many people are on the case, for* | *1.* **Integrity** *(being honest, even when no one is watching)*<br>Straightforward and honest in all professional and business relationships, fair dealing and truthfulness.<br>*2.* **Objectivity**( *not to take any sides, so maintain independent decision making)*<br>Do not to compromise the profession or business judgment because of bias, conflict of interest or the undue influence of others.<br>*3.* **Professional competence and due care** *(not to bring the reputation of accounting into disrepute)*<br>Maintain professional knowledge and skill and to act diligently, in accordance with applicable technical and professional.<br>*4.* **Confidentiality** *(not to be going discussing clients private matters with third parties" unless legally bound")*<br>Keep information confidential; take all reasonable steps to preserve confidentiality. Ensure all unpublished information about a client's or employer's affairs are confidential.<br>*5.* **Professional behaviour** *(to stay inside the law and to ensure that policies and best practice are adhered to)*<br>Comply with relevant laws and regulations and avoid any action that may discredit or adversely affect the |

| | |
|---|---|
| *instance, only sending four people when ten is needed, to save costs.* *The firm cannot charge a contingent fee, meaning they cannot charge a fee which is based on the audit outcome.* *The firm must remove themselves from the audit of there is any litigation between themselves or the client or any subsidiaries.* *Firms are not allowed to accept gifts or hospitality from the client; this can impair judgement in independence.* **5. Non-Audit services provided to Audit Clients** *Firms should not (excluding small entities) undertake external services or non-audit services to clients, including internal audits, tax services, accounting, and IT services. This is to ensure objectivity, independence and integrity remains at the core of the firm. (small entities can use exemption to no5, so long as they disclose it an put it on the auditor's report)* | good reputation of the profession |

## Ethical Conflict Resolution

Where a conflict of interest poses a threat to one or more of the fundamental principles, including objectivity, confidentiality or professional behaviour, that cannot be eliminated or reduced to an acceptable level through the application of safeguards, the member in public practice shall conclude that it is not appropriate to accept a specific engagement or that resignation from one or more conflicting engagements is required.

**The ethical conflict resolution process.**

A member may be required to resolve a conflict in complying with the fundamental principles. When initiating either a formal or informal conflict resolution process, a member shall consider the following, either individually or together with others, as part of the resolution process:

(a) Relevant facts;

(b) Ethical issues involved;

(c) Fundamental principles related to the matter in question;

(d) Established internal procedures; and

(e) Alternative courses of action.

After considering the issue, an auditor is expected to determine the best course of action, and that this action is consistent with the fundamental principles, while considering the consequences of each action they take. If the matter persists then the auditor should speak to another member of their firm (if they have any) or seeking external resolution experts.

If the conflict is within the organisation itself then the auditor should discuss these issues with the governance board. The auditor should write down all relevant information and keep records of any issues which arise, and all discussion and meeting which took place regard the issue.

If a resolution cannot be reached within the organisation itself the auditor should seek advice from a professional body or legal advisor, this ensure that the accountant receives advice on the best course of action without the concern of breaching confidentially. After seeking this advice the auditor can determine if they are under an obligation to report.

If the issue is still not resolved after all of the above steps are taken, the auditor may decide that stepping down from the assignment, or the organisation itself is the best option for them.

## Using the services of an external Expert

### Using the work of an expert o

When considering using the services of an expert the auditor should agree the nature and objectives in securing the services of the expert, what roles they will fulfil and their responsibilities of that position.

There are specific requirements which must be agreed before the expert is hired, such as

- the nature, timing and extent of communication between the two parties, and
- the need for the expert to observe confidentiality

The Auditor must also determine the processes they will use in evaluating the expert's work, the consistency of the expert's findings with the other audit evidence. The auditor must also consider the use and accuracy of source data which the expert uses. An auditor might rely on an expert's finding when they need a/an:

- valuation of a non-current asset

- inventory counts or valuations
- legal opinions
- actuarial valuations e.g. on payment in future, such as retirement funds.

The expert's objectivity and professional competence needs to be assessed in order to determine if the work of the expert is adequate.

1. When the auditor has reason to believe an illegal act has occurred, they should:
   a) inquire of management at a level above, those likely to be involved with the illegality.
   b) consider accumulating additional evidence to determine if there is actually an illegal act.
   c) consult with the client's legal advisors.
   d) all of the above

2. If the auditor believes that the financial statements are not fairly stated or if they are unable to reach a conclusion because of insufficient evidence, the auditor:
   a) should withdraw from the engagement.
   b) should request an increase in audit fees so that more resources can be used to conduct the audit.
   c) has the responsibility of notifying financial statement users through the auditor's report.
   d) report the client to the audit committee

3. The responsibility for adopting sound accounting policies and maintaining adequate internal controls in accounting practices is the responsibility of the:
   a) board of directors.
   b) company management.
   c) financial statement auditor.
   d) company's internal audit department

4. The responsibility of the presentation of a fair and accurate financial statement lies jointly with the management and the auditors,
   a) true
   b) false

5. Which of the following statements is most correct regarding errors and fraud?
   a) an error is unintentional, whereas fraud is intentional.
   b) frauds occur more often than errors in financial statements.
   c) errors are always fraud and frauds are always errors.
   d) auditors have more responsibility for detecting fraud than correcting it

6. Where an auditor uncovers fraud by management which was unintentional and accidental, this leaves them unaccountable for any fraudulent activity,?

a) true
b) false

7. Which of the following is the auditor least likely to do when aware of an illegal act?
   a) discuss the matter with the client's legal advisors
   b) obtain evidence about the potential effect of the illegal act on the financial statements.
   c) contact the Gardaí regarding potential legal consequences
   d) report the matter to the inland revenue

8. An auditor must not assume their client in inherently dishonest, however they must consider that this is a possibility, this would be classed as:
   a) unprofessional behaviour.
   b) an attitude of professional scepticism.
   c) due diligence.
   d) a rule in the IFAC's Code of Professional Conduct

9. If a number of employees decided amongst themselves to perpetrate fraud in the accounting, would this be a relatively easy for the auditor to detect?
   a) yes
   b) no

10.    The difference between an accountant and an auditor is, the accountant must possess the standards a reasonable accountant, and apply this knowledge to producing the financial statements of a company. Whereas the auditor must be an expert accountant giving them the knowledge and experience  so that they can assess the standards of accounting and make an informed decision about the accuracy of the financial statements.
   a) true
   b) false

## Solutions to Multiple Choice Questions

1. An example of a change in the Constitution is
   **a) Abolition of the death Penalty 2001**
   b) Cigarette penalties 2004
   c) Abolition of free plastic bags in shops 2003
   d) New President

2. In 1972 an amendment to the Irish Constitution lowered the voting age to
   a) 19
   b) 21
   **c) 18**
   d) 16

3. What is the "burden of proof" that the prosecution has to establish for a jury to convict a defendant in Irish criminal cases?
   a) on the balance of probabilities
   b) depending on intention
   c) beyond all doubt
   **d) beyond reasonable doubt**

4. In which court will a case be brought against a defendant for speeding, TV licence or drink driving?
   a) District Court
   **b) District Criminal Court**
   c) Circuit Civil Court
   d) Circuit Criminal Court

5. What is the Statute of limitations for the tort of Negligence?
   a) 1 year
   **b) 2 years**
   c) 3 years
   d) 6 years

6. What is the Statute of limitations for the tort of Nuisance?
   a) 1 year
   b) 2 years
   c) 3 years
   **d) 6 years**

7. An example of Irish Secondary legislation is;
   a) The Road Traffic Act
   b) The Consumer Protection Act
   c) Hiways and Byways Protection
   **d) Construction Regulations 2006–2012**

8. Where does the European Commission have its offices?
   a) Dublin
   b) London
   c) Luxemburg
   **d) Brussels**

9. An example of EU Secondary legislation is;
   a) The Road Traffic Act
   b) The Consumer Protection Act
   c) Hiways and Byways Protection
   **d) European Union (Batteries and Accumulators) Regulation.**

10. Ireland joined the EU in?
    **a) 1973**
    b) 1959
    c) 1981
    d) 1990

11. The Supreme court in Ireland is the highest court in Ireland dealing with:
    a) National issues
    b) EU issues
    c) All issues
    **d) Appeals cases only**

12. A jury can be used in civil cases in Ireland where the case is a case on
    a) Negligence
    b) Nuisance
    **c) Defamation**
    d) Trespass

13. Which of the following is associated with private law?
    a) Constitution law
    b) Criminal law
    **c) Civil law**
    d) None of the above

14. Which of the following courts in the Irish legal system has criminal jurisdiction?

a) District Civil Court
**b) Central Criminal Court**
c) Court of Civil Appeal
d) Circuit Court

15.     Dan has been stopped for drunk driving, he is legally over the limit, and has been charged under the Road Traffic Act, he is fighting this case as he claims his car works on auto pilot and therefore the is not actually driving it, which statutory interpretation would the judge most likely use in this case to ensure that the law was adhered to?
a) Literal rule
b) Golden rule
**c) Mischief rule**
d) Ejusdem Generis rule

16.     Which of the following terms best describes the reason for the judge's decision?
a) Per incuriam
b) Obiter dicta
**c) Ratio decidendi**
d) None of the Above

17.     Which rule of interpretation involves an examination of the intention of the Oireachtas?
a) The golden rule
b) The literal rule
**c) The mischief rule**
d) The obiter rule

18.     Which of the following describes a statement that is made obiter dicta?
a) It is binding on all lower courts hearing similar cases
b) It is not binding unless made by the Supreme court
**c) It is a statement made by the judge when summing up**
d) None of the Above

19.     Those who come to equity must come with clean hands." – this is a _____.
a) Precedent
**b) Maxim of equity**
c) Obiter dictum
d) All of the above

20.     Which of the following is a maxim of equity
**a) Those who seek equity must not do impersoram**

b) Those who come to equity may have dirty hands
c) **Equity aids the vigilant not those who sleep on their rights**
d) Those who come to equity must do so vigilantly

21. Which of the following is NOT an equitable remedy
   a) Injunction
   b) Rescission
   **c) Damages**
   d) Mareva

22. Which of the following is a common law remedy
   a) Specific performance
   b) Rectification
   **c) Damages**
   d) Injunction

23. The modern Irish legal system came about when which systems combined
   a) Brehon laws and Common law
   b) **Equity and Common law**
   c) Brehon Law and Equity
   d) Civil law and common law

24. The Oireachtas get its power to create legislation from;
   a) statute law
   b) precedent
   **c) the constitution**
   d) all of the above

25. The two main divisions of law are
   a) Constitution law and statute
   b) Criminal law and statute
   **c) Criminal law and civil law**
   d) Civil law and Constitutional law

26. The major differences between civil and criminal law is
   **a) Civil law's burden of proof is less than criminal law**
   b) Civil law has the same burden of proof as criminal law
   c) Criminal law's burden of proof is less than civil law
   d) Criminal law has no burden of proof, only standard of proof

27. The role of the victim in a criminal trial is as;
   a) prosecution
   b) defendant
   **c) witness**

d) none of the above

28. A custodial sentence is a punishments for an offender who is guilty of;
   a) **a criminal offence**
   b) a breach of a consumer contract
   c) not getting required planning permission
   d) exceeding the agreed expenditure on sales contracts

29. The Burden of Proof means
   a) The difficulties in proving the facts of the case
   b) **The party who has to prove the facts of the case**
   c) The amount of evidence the parties are required to have
   d) None of the above

30. What is the standard of proof in civil law
   a) beyond reasonable doubt
   b) **balance of probabilities**
   c) what the judge believes
   d) what is fair just and reasonable

31. The standard of proof in criminal law is
   a) balance of probabilities
   b) the best evidence presented
   c) **beyond reasonable doubt**
   d) what the legal teams produce to court

32. The liable party will have to
   a) **Paying compensation**
   b) Have a custodial sentence
   c) Serve community service
   d) Be put on probation

33. The Oireachtas is made up of
   a) Courts, Dáil and President
   b) **Dáil, Seanad and President**
   c) Uachtaran na hÉireann, Dáil and Courts
   d) Seanad and Dáil

34. A Bill can only become law when it has passed by
   a) The Dáil
   b) The Seanad
   c) **The Dáil and the Seanad**
   d) The President

35.　　　When a Bill becomes a law it is called
   **a) Act of the Oireachtas**
   b) Statute
   c) Presidential Bill
   d) a and b

36.　　　The literal rule means that the judge will interpret the Statue to mean
   a) what the legislature intended
   b) what the legal teams agreed to
   **c) the ordinary meaning of the words used**
   d) none of the above

37.　　　The golden rule means that the judge will interpret the Statue to mean
   a) what the legislature intended
   **b) the interpretation of the words in the statute**
   c) the argument put forward by counsel
   d) none of the above

38.　　　Under European Law a European Directive
   **a) is implemented into national law by an act of the Oireachtas**
   b) only needs implementation should Ireland wish to
   c) is directly effective from Europe as soon as it is passed
   d) all of the above

39.　　　Under European Law a European Regulation
   a) is implemented by an Act of the Oireachtas
   **b) is directly binding on Ireland when it is passed in Europe**
   c) is implemented on a stage basis by Ireland
   d) none of the above

40.　　　The decisions of courts outside of Ireland are
   a) binding
   b) original
   **c) persuasive**
   d) dissenting

41.　　　The courts of first instance in Ireland are
   a) District Court and Supreme Court
   **b) District Court, Circuit Court and High Court**
   c) Central Criminal Court and the Court of Appeal
   d) The Special Criminal Court and the Supreme Court

42. The highest Court in Ireland is
   a) Court of Appeal
   b) Circuit Court
   **c) Supreme Court**
   d) The District Court

43. You have been arrested on a summary offence.  This means that
   a) the case will be heard by a judge sitting alone
   b) the case will be heard by a judge and jury
   c) the maximum sentence is 12 months
   d) the sentenced will be a minimum of 24 months
      1. A only
      **2. A and c**
      3. C only

44. The accused solicitor has told them that their offence is an indictable offence tried summarily, this means:
   a) it is a serious offence tried in the District Court before a judge and jury
   b) it is a minor offence tried in the Circuit Court with a judge sitting alone with no jury
   **c) it is an offence which is indictable in nature, but with the client and prosecution's consent it can be heard by the District Court judge**
   d) it is an offence which is summary in nature, and with the defence's consent it can be heard by the District Court judge

45. Where a court applies a precedent from another Jurisdiction, this precedent is said to be
   a) Binding
   b) Authorative
   **c) Persuasive**
   d) Permissible

46. A statutory instrument is
   a) Primary legislation
   **b) Secondary/delegated legislation**
   c) Common law legislation
   d) Precedent

47. A European Directive
   **a) Is the will of the EU implemented by each Country in their own terms**
   b) Has no requirement to be enacted into Irish law by the Oireachtas

c) Has direct effect into Irish law as soon as it is passed in Europe
d) All of the above

48. The Courts of First Instance in Ireland are
   a) Where the legal proceedings are finalised
   **b) Where the legal proceedings are initiated**
   c) Where the parties can appeal a decision
   d) None of the above

49. Where the accused is sentenced in the District Court and they appeal their case, if they lose this case, their maximum sentence will be
   a) 6 months
   **b) 12 months**
   c) 24 months
   d) 9 months

50. Where the damages in a personal injury case are estimated at €60,500, the case will be heard in the;
   a) Circuit Criminal Court
   b) District Court
   c) Circuit Civil Court
   **d) High Court**

## Solutions to Multiple Choice Questions

1.     What is the standard of care applied to professionals with a special skill or expertise?
   a) That of the reasonable person with the same skill or expertise
   b) That of the reasonable person in that profession
   c) That of the reasonably qualified person
   **d) That of the reasonable person with the same level of experience or skill in that profession.**

2.     What does a claimant need to show to establish liability in a negligence claim?
   1. There was a duty of care
   2. That the duty was not breached
   3. The breach caused damage
   4. The damage was foreseeable
      a. 1, 2 and 4 only
      **b. 1, 3 and 4 only**
      c. 2 and 3 only
      d. All of the above

3.     What does the "*eggshell skull*" rule mean?
   a) That defendant is not liable where the plaintiff had a pre-existing injury
   **b) That defendants must take their victims as they find them**
   c) The defendant is liable for injuries which would be foreseen by a reasonable person
   d) None of the above

4.     Which of the following may give rise to vicarious liability?
   1. Vehicle owners and their permitted drivers.
   2. Employer and employee.
   3. Teachers and pupils in their care during school hours.
      **a. 1 and 2 only**
      b. 1 and 3 only
      c. 2 and 3 only
      d. 1, 2 and 3 only

5.     Which case ruled that where a person who is visiting a house, acts on the instruction of the owner of the property, the owner is liable for their acts?

a) Re Polomis
b) Hadley v Baxendale
c) Speight V Gosnay
d) **Moynihan v Moynihan**

6. Define the meaning of the defence *volenti non fit injuria*?
   a) **There is no liability on the defendant where the plaintiff has voluntary assumed the risk**
   b) The person who causes the injury must be held liable
   c) The compensation must fit the damages
   d) None of the above

7. Where a defendant can prove contributory negligence against the plaintiff, they are proving
   a) The plaintiff did not contribute to their own injuries
   b) The defendant contributed to the plaintiffs injuries
   c) **The plaintiff contributed to their own injuries**
   d) None of the above

8. Sarah is learning to drive; she is negligent and mounts the kerb, injuring her driving instructor, what is Sarah's duty of care in this case
   a) There is a driver to driver duty of care owed
   b) **The duty owed is that of a reasonable learner driver**
   c) The duty of care is that owed by a learner driver
   d) All of the Above

9. Interference with another's enjoyment of life or property is known as:
   a) Trespass
   b) **Nuisance**
   c) Defamation
   d) None of the above

10. A wrongful act that injures another's reputation with false statements is known as:
    a) Trespass
    b) Nuisance
    c) **Defamation**
    d) None of the above

11. The failure to exercise the degree of care that a reasonable person would exercise those results in the proximate cause of actual harm to an innocent person is known as:
    a) Strict Liability
    b) Nuisance
    c) Defamation
    d) **Negligence**

12.    The tort that results when one person deliberately frightens another person into the reasonable belief that he or she is about to be injured is known as:
   a) **Assault**
   b) Battery
   c) Assault and Battery
   d) Grievous bodily harm

13.    Manufacturers product Strict Liability requires
   a) Fault
   b) **No fault**
   c) Damage
   d) None of the above

14.    The rule in *__Mc Kenna V Best travel__* stated that
   a) There were liable as they had brought the defendant to a dangerous territory
   b) They were not liable as they had got the plaintiff to sign a disclaimer before leaving
   c) **There were not guilty as they had no specialised knowledge of the risks**
   d) They were not guilty as the plaintiff had voluntarily went to the danger

15.    The requirement that, the damage need not be foreseeable was a ruling in the case of:
   a) **Hadley v Baxendale**
   b) Carlill v Carbolic smokeball
   c) Re Polomis
   d) Quigley v Creation

16.    The court ruling in *Speight v Gosnay* stated that:
   a) Where a statement lowers the applicant in the eyes of a community the defendant is liable in defamation
   b) The applicant can bring a case in defamation if they receive a defamatory letter from an individual; they are the only ones to read it.
   c) The defendant is liable if the plaintiff reads the defamatory statement and is upset
   d) **The defendant is liable if another person republishes the defamatory statement even if it is withdrawn by the original poster**

17.    Liquidated damages are
   a) **Quantifiable**

    b) Unquantifiable
    c) Unknown
    d) None of the above

18. ***Grant v Australian Knitting Mills*** involved which Tort:
    **a) Negligence**
    b) Nuisance
    c) Defamation
    d) Assault

19. The Irish precedent case in defining the Duty of Care owed is:
    a) Donoghue v Stevenson
    b) Carlill v Carbolic Smokeball
    **c) Glencar v Mayo Co Co**
    d) Caparo Industries v Dickman Plc.

20. Remoteness of damages can be defined as:
    a) Proximity of the parties
    b) Duty of care owed
    **c) Reasonable Foreseeability**
    d) Standard of Care

21. Which of the following is a defence in Nuisance
    a) It is a quarry, there will be noise
    b) The levels of noise are acceptable
    **c) Prescription**
    d) All of the above

22. Strict liability occurs when;
    **a) There is no requirement to find fault**
    b) Fault must be established
    c) Fault is established one the duty of care is established
    d) The parties agree there is fault

23. The tort of passing off occurs when
    a) A seller sells his own goods on his own market stalls
    **b) A seller sells goods and leads buyers to believe they are the goods of a competitor**
    c) A buyer believes the goods on sale are branded goods and buys them
    d) A seller tells the buyer the goods look like those of a competitor but they are not

24. Interference with another's enjoyment of life or property is known as
    a) Defamation

b) Tort
c) Trespass to the Person
**d) Nuisance**

25. The tort of Conversion is defined as;
a) a person lending a neighbour their lawnmower
**b) taking another person property and using for personal gain**
c) giving property back to the owner when they ask for it
d) none of the above

26. The tort that results when one person deliberately frightens another person into the reasonable belief that he or she is about to be injured is known as:
a) conversion
b) tort
**c) assault**
d) battery

27. Failure to return goods to the owner when requested is called;
a) conversion
b) nuisance
c) trespass to the person
**d) detinue**

28. Prescription is a defence to
**a) nuisance**
b) trespass to land
c) nuisance
d) defamation

29. Statutory Authority gets its power from
**a) legislation**
b) common law
c) prescription
d) case law

30. *Res Ipsa Loquitur* means.
a) the solicitor speaks with the prosecution
**b) the thing speaks for itself**
c) the defendant speaks for themself
d) the barrister speaks for the defendant

31. Liability for dangerous or "unnatural things" stems from the case of;
a) Donoghue v Stevenson
b) Hadley v Baxendale
c) Quigley v Creation

**d) Rylands v Fletcher**

32.   Despite the defendant not having done anything wrong, they may still be held liable in tort under:

    a) negligence
    **b) strict liability**
    c) defamation
    d) trespass

33.   An employer's liability for the actions of their employee, who is acting outside the scope of their employment, or outside their working time, has;

    a) vicarious liability
    **b) no liability**
    c) employers liability
    d) employees' rights at work

34.   Slander is defined as;
    **a) the spoken word**
    b) the written word
    c) words found online
    d) none of the above

35.   Libel is defined as;
    a) the spoken word
    **b) the written word**
    c) words found online
    d) none of the above

36.   In defamation, opinions are *generally*
    a) actionable
    **b) non actionable**
    c) libellous
    d) slanderous

37.   In defamation, republication is actionable as per;
    **a) Quigley v Creation**
    b) Speight v Gosney
    c) Donoghue v Stevenson
    d) Hadley v Baxendale

38.   To be defamatory, a statement must,
    a) be told to the defendant
    b) be told to the general public
    **c) be communicated to a third party**
    d) be thought by the defendant

39.   Which case laid down the precedent in determining the duty of care?
    **a)  Donoghue v Stevenson**

   b) Fischer v bell
   c) Caparo Industries v Dickman Plc.
   d) Partridge v Crittenden

40.   Mitigation of losses means;
   a) The defendant must take reasonable care to ensure they do not damage the plaintiff's goods
   **b) The plaintiff must take reasonable steps to reduce their own losses**
   c) The plaintiff must take every step possible to reduce their own losses
   d) The defendant must take reasonable steps to reduce their plaintiff's losses

41.   Which of the following cases resulted in the court finding that cost of avoiding the risk outweighed the risk and found that the defendant was not negligent.
   a) The Wagon Mound 2
   **b) Latimer v AEC**
   c) Donoghue v Stevenson
   d) Caparo Industries v Dickman Plc.

42.   The case of **McGhee v National Coal Board** is relevant to
   a) The "but for" test
   b) Causation
   c) Remoteness of damage
   **d) Material contribution test**

43.   Which of the following is NOT a type of damages
   a) Nominal damages
   b) Exemplary damages
   c) Aggravated damages
   **d) Contemporary damages**

44.   Which case was the claimant found to have contributed to their injuries
   a) Livox Quarries v Boyce
   b) Jones v Boyce
   **c) Jones v Livox Quarries**
   d) Smith v Jones

45.   Contributory negligence occurs when:
   a) The plaintiff was hurt because of the actions of the defendant
   b) The plaintiff was a reasonable person who was hurt due to another's actions

c) **The plaintiff was wholly or partly to blame for their own injuries**

d) The plaintiff was an innocent victim in an accident

46. How does the courts best determine if an employer is vicariously liable for the actions of staff?
    a) **Is the employee carrying out an authorised act**
    b) The reasonable man test
    c) Proximity test
    d) Fair just and reasonable

47. What is the closest description of the *reasonable man*
    a) He is very cautious
    b) He is very safety conscious
    c) He was low intelligence
    d) **He is neither very cautious nor does he take excessive risks**

48. Vicariously liable' means
    a) **A person is responsible for another's actions**
    b) A person is not responsible for another's actions
    c) A person is responsible for their own actions
    d) None Of The Above

49. What is the purpose of determining if a duty of care exists
    a) To ensure that all parties are treated fairly
    b) **To determine who is liable for the damage**
    c) It ensure that the right person is sued
    d) To determine if the wrongdoer was actually careless

50. Why did Mrs Donoghue bring an action in tort and not in contract?
    a) **She was not a party to the contract and therefore the only avenue was tort**
    b) She had a contract which was frustrated so had to bring an action in tort
    c) She had the ginger beer drank before she seen the snail so contract was discharged
    d) She bought the ginger beer with her friends money so she had no contract

## Solutions to Multiple Choice Questions

Section Three – LO3 MCQs

1.     Sarah goes into a shop and sees a price label on a CD for €5. She takes the CD to the checkout, but the checkout operator tells her that the label is misprinted and should read €15. Sarah maintains that she only has to pay €5.
How would you describe the price on the label in terms of contract law?
   a) Sarah has a contract as the price is clearly stated
   **b) Sarah has no contract, as this is an invitation to treat**
   c) Sarah has no contract as she did not offer the store the €5
   d) None of the above

2.     Minimum wage in Ireland is:
   **a) €9.25**
   b) €8.64
   c) €8.50
   d) €11.50

3.     The case of **_Fisher v Bell_** in contract law dealt with
   e) Offers
   **a) Invitations to treat**
   b) Consideration
   c) Intention to Create Legal Relations

4.     Which of the following statements is/are correct?
   1. A term inserted into a contract attempting to exclude liability for damage to property caused by negligence is void unless it is reasonable.
   2. An exclusion clause which attempts to exclude liability for death or personal injury is void.
   a) 1 only
   **b) 2 only**
   c) Neither 1 nor 2
   d) Both 1 and 2

5.     James sent a letter to Sarah offering to sell Sarah his motorbike for €3,000.  Sarah wrote back saying she accepted the offer and would pay in two instalments at the end of the two following months.
**Does Sarah have a contract with James?**
   **a) No – because Sarah is trying to amend the terms.**

b) Yes – there has been an offer and acceptance and a binding contract exists

c) No – Sarah's response constitutes a counter-offer and is voids the original offer.

d) Yes – Sarah's response is merely a clarification of contractual terms

6.     Stan made an offer by letter posted which he posted on 15th January and delivered on 18th January. Jackie's replied accepting the offer was mailed on 19th January and the Stan received it on 20th January. Stan read the reply on 25th of January. **On which date was the contract made?**

a) 15th January

b) 18th January

**c) 19th January**

d) 25th January

7.     Sam put his computer for sale in his shop window, the sign says "*special offer, computer for sale, €500.00*". **Which of the following is correct?**

a) This is an offer, and Sam must sell it to anyone who comes in and asks for it at that price.

b) This is an invitation to treat only, as per Partridge v Crittenden

**c) This is an invitation to treat only, as per Fischer v Bell**

d) This is an offer as per Carlill v Carbolic Smokeball

8.     Mary owed John €2,000. Mary's father, Thomas, agreed with John, in writing, to pay him €1,200 if he took it "*in full settlement*". John took the €1,200 on this basis and then demanded €800.00 from Mary. Mary has refused to pay.

**Explain Mary's position?**

a) Mary is liable – part payment of a debt is not consideration for a promise to discharge the debt

**b) Mary is not liable – part payment of a debt by a third party is good consideration for a promise not to sue for the balance**

c) Mary will be liable – Thomas, as her father, is not a third party

d) Mary will not be liable – the agreement between John and Thomas was in writing

9.     The law in relation to the "intention to create legal relations" in social and domestic situations, presumes that there is:

1. An intention to create legal relations

2. No intention to create legal relations

3. An intention unless the presumption can be rebutted

4. No intention unless it is in writing

a) 1 and 2 only

b) 1 and 3 only

**c) 2 and 4 only**

d) All of the above

10. Steven is 25 years old, he has just started his first job after college, and he has not worked before this time. **Steven is entitled under the Payment of Wages Act to:**

    a) €9.25 ph.

    **b) €7.40 ph.**

    c) €6.48 ph.

    d) €8.33 ph.

11. Jack has been working for 117 hours since he started working in his new job, he now requires a week off as holidays, **and how much holiday pay is Jack entitled to?**

    a) 2 working weeks

    b) 1/3 of a working week

    c) 9% of the total hours worked to date

    **d) None of the above**

12. Susie offered to sell her car to Scott for €2,000 on January the 5th, Scott replied to this offer asking her if the car had been serviced and did it need new tyres. Susie replied on the 6th of January, it had new tyres and was serviced recently and said she would keep the offer open until the 10th of January. Scott contacted Susie on the 8th of January and told her he would give her €1,500 for the car, on the 9th of January, Jane bought the car from Susie. When Scott arrived to Susie's house on the 10th with €2,000, he was told it was sold. **Explain the legal position of Susie and Scott**

    a) There is a contract to sell at €2,000, so Scott may recover the car from Susie as it is now his property

    b) When Susie sold the car to Jane, she voided the contract with Scott

    c) There is an offer from Susie to sell to Scott for €2,000 which is still open until the 10th for Scott to accept

    **d) There is no contract between Susie and Scott as Scott terminated the offer with Susie when he counter offered €1,500**

13. In which of the following circumstances is there an intention to create legal relations

    a) Taking your friends dog for a walk

    **b) Taking your friends children to school, you have a contract, you are their paid child-minder**

    c) Taking your friends children to school as a favour

    d) None of the above

14.    Jacob owes Andrew €1,000, this is to be paid by August the 1st, On July 15th Jacob send Andrew a cheque for €750.00 in *full and final payment* of the debt, Andrew lodged the cheque into his bank account, **explain If Andrew can sue Jacob for the €250.00**
   a) **Yes, since part payment of a debt cannot provide satisfaction for the agreement to discharge the debt**
   b) No, because Andrew by his promise will be estopped from insisting on his legal rights
   c) Yes, since the payment of €750.00 on the 15th of July is not adequate consideration for the promise not to sue
   d) No, because part payment early at the request of Andrew provides satisfaction for the agreement to discharge the debt

15.    **Which of the following statements are correct?**
   1. A condition is a term which is fundamental to the contract, the contract is void if a condition is breached
   2. A warranty is not fundamental to the contract, the contract is not void if a warranty is breached
   3. If an innominate term is broken the innocent party has the option whether or not to terminate the contract.
      a) 1 only
      b) 1 and 2 only
      c) 2 and 3 only
      d) **1, 2 and 3**

16.    **An unclear or ambiguous term in a contract is:**
   a) **Contra Proferentum and goes against the person relying on the contract**
   b) Contra Proferentum and goes in favour of the person relying on the contract
   c) Volenti non fit injura and goes in favour of the person relying on it
   d) Unconscionable bargain and goes against the person replying on it

17.    A contract which lacks legal formality is
   a) Void
   b) Voidable
   c) **Unenforceable**
   d) All of the above

18.    Maria went to the cinema last week, she was queuing to get her ticket and noticed a sign over the counter in the cinema which stated, *management accept no liability for any injuries howsoever caused*, Maria

tripped on a piece of carpet which was sticking up when she was leaving the cinema. **Explain Maria's legal position**

    a) She can bring a case for personal injury as she wasn't wearing her glasses and wasn't able to read the sign.

    b) She cannot bring a personal injury case as the sign clearly stated in advance that the management accepted no liability

    **c) She can bring a personal injury case as no liability can be excluded for negligence**

    d) None of the above

19. Which of the follow does **<u>not</u>** allow the innocent party to repudiate the contract?

    a) A condition

    **b) A warranty**

    c) An innominate term

    d) None of the above

20. In terms of the law of contract, **which of the following statements is correct?**

    a) A breach of an innominate term automatically voids the contract

    b) A breach of a warranty entitles the innocent part to repudiate the contract

    **c) A breach of a condition automatically voids a contract**

    d) A breach of a condition makes the contract voidable

21. Mikov, a wholesaler; he orders 10 crates of lager with 24 bottles in each from his off licence, he receives all 240 bottles of lager, but in crates with different quantities in them. Mikov rejects the whole order, **what is Mikov's liability in contract law?**

    **a) There is no breach of condition or warranty as this is not a consumer sale, therefore Mikov is liable for breach of contract**

    b) There has only been a breach of warranty, therefore Mikov must pay and claim damages

    c) Mikov is in breach of contract by rejecting the goods and is liable to pay damages

    d) There has been a breach of condition that the goods match the description, therefore Mikov is entitled to treat the contract as discharged

22. **What does a breach of a condition entitle the injured party to do?**

    a) Claim damages only

    b) Sue on a quantum meruit

    **c) Repudiate the contract and claim damages**

    d) None of the above

23.   Which of the following contracts would be enforceable by specific performance

    **a) A plumber who has agreed to the terms of the contract and not started the job**
    b) A tiller who has started work and has had an accident leaving him out of work for a year
    c) A minor
    d) A contract for the payment of a deposit

24.   Where the seller delivers goods which are **<u>less</u>** than the quantity ordered amount the buyer may:

    **a) Either reject them or accept the short delivery and pay pro-rata for the goods that have been delivered**
    b) Either reject or accept them. If he accepts them, he must pay the full contract price
    c) The buyer must reject the whole consignment
    d) The buyer must accept the whole consignment

25.   Where the seller delivers goods which are **<u>more</u>** than the quantity ordered amount the buyer may:

    a) The buyer may accept the correct quantity and reject the remainder
    **b) The buyer may accept the correct quantity and reject the remainder, OR may reject the entire delivery**
    c) The buyer must accept the entire consignment
    d) The buyer must reject the entire consignment

26.   The duty on a party to mitigate their losses means:

    a) They have a duty to ensure they get as much compensation as the law will allow
    b) They have a right to compensation for foreseeable damages caused
    **c) They are required to reduce the impact and losses which they incur**
    d) None of the above

27.   Where there has been a breach of contract, the court must award one of the following:

    a) Specific performance
    **b) Damages**
    c) Injunctions
    d) All of the above

28.   What is the equitable remedy of recession?

    **a) The contract never existed**

b) Changes to the contract
c) Compensation to the injured party
d) None of the above

29. The court in the case of **Stilk v Myrich** ruled that:
   **a) No extra consideration was given by the crew, therefore no money was payable**
   b) Extra consideration was given as the crew had come back with the ship as promised
   c) Consideration was given as the they were promised the money
   d) None of the above

30. In the case of **Hartley v Ponsoby** the court ruled:
   e) No extra consideration was given by the crew, therefore no money was payable
   **a) Extra consideration was given as the crew; they had done extra work and gone beyond their contractual duties.**
   b) Consideration was given as the they were promised the money
   c) None of the above

31. Intention to create legal relation in the case of **Edwards v Skyways**, was
   **a) Proven as intention is implied in commercial contracts, even if signed otherwise**
   b) Not proven, as there was no intention as Edwards had signed a contract station it was "ex gratia" and no intention existed
   c) Edwards had signed a contract stating there was no intention, this inserted an exclusion clause
   d) None of the above

32. The Enterprise test in defining whether a worker is as employee or self-employed contractor investigates:
   1. If the employer decides the hours and place of work of the employee
   2. If the worker has to attend meetings and is given expenses to cover diesel or petrol
   3. If the worker is allowed to work for other companies while worker for employer.
   4. If the worker has the power to instruct another worker to take over their job on their behalf.
      a) 1 only
      b) 1 and 4
      **c) 3 and 4**
      d) 2 and 3

33.    The control test in defining if a worker is employed or self-employed is defined:

    **a) If the employer decides the hours and place of work of the employee**

    b) If the worker has to attend meetings and is given expenses to cover diesel or petrol

    c) If the worker is allowed to work for other companies while worker for employer.

    d) If the worker has the power to instruct another worker to take over their job on their behalf.

34.    When defining consideration in a contract, which of the following is **not** good consideration

    1. A father telling his son he will pay him to stop complaining,

    2. A son promising to stop complaining if his father pays him money

    3. A son asking his father how much is it worth for him to stop complaining

    4. None of the above

        a.  1 only

        **b.  1 and 2 only**

        c.  1, 2 and 3

        d.  1 and 3 only

35.    The case of **Whyte v Bluett** concerned

    a) A self-employed contractor claiming he was an employee

    **b) A father offering to pay his son to stop complaining**

    c) A son offering to stop complaining if he got paid

    d) A worker who was defined as self-employed as he could get another worker to take his place

36.    Which case defined the principle that where a party provides more than an existing duty requires them to do, they can look for extra payment?

    a) Whyte v Bluett

    b) Fischer v Bell

    c) Edwards v Skyways

    **d) Glasbrook Bros v Glamorgan City Council**

37.    In the case of **Harvella Investments v Royal Trust Company** the courts stated that:

    a) A price need not be agreed in order for referential bids to be accepted

    **b) Referential bids are not acceptable, as a price needs to be stated**

    c) Referential bids are not legally binding

    d) None of the above

38. An implied contract is one where:
    a) The parties must state the terms of the contract
    **b) The terms do not need to be written down, they can be unspoken, unwritten**
    c) Silence does not constitute acceptance
    d) None of the above

39. The case of **Spurling v Bradshaw** defined the principle that
    a) A contract is void if it is signed after the agreement is made
    b) A contract is valid even if it is signed after the agreement is made
    **c) A contract is valid if it is signed after it is made, as long as the parties have previous dealings**
    d) A contract is not valid if it is signed after it is made, even if the parties have previous dealings

40. When one party to a contract states before it starts that they will not be able to perform the contract his breach is called
    **a) Anticipatory breach**
    b) Repudiatory breach
    c) Liquidated breach
    d) Fundamental breach

41. Motorway Builder Ltd agreed to build a new road for XCity to be completed on 15 March 2017. The contract provided for a penalty of €1,000 per day from 15 March to date of actual completion.
The road was 20 days late and as a result XCity was able to prove that they had lost
€60,000 of revenue and €5,000 of profits in the St Patrick's Day period.
**What is the maximum amount XCity may recover from Motorway Builder Ltd?**
    a) Nil
    **b) €20,000**
    c) €50,000
    d) €65,000

42. What is the Statute of Limitation for breach of a simple contract?
    a) 1 year
    b) 2 years
    c) 3 years
    **d) 6 years**

43. Michael, an estate agent in Dublin has on his books two houses for sale, Mark isn't sure which one to buy as he likes both of them, he reads the brochures for both houses and decided to go with house B, as the garden in

house B is bigger than the garden of house A.  The brochure states that the garden in house A is 30m x 10m and the garden in house B is 40m x 10m, both houses are in the same street and house B is 5k cheaper.   Michael goes to view house B, but it is dark and he only looks into the garden, and doesn't measure it, he buys house B and subsequently finds out that the garden is in fact 30m x 10 m and not 40m x 10m as stated in the brochure, he is considering suing the estate agent, he asks for your advice. **Explain to Michael if the wrong size in the brochure was a:**
- a) Condition
- b) Warranty
- **c) Representation**
- d) Innominate term

44.   A common mistake occurs when
- a) Both parties are mistaken about different terms in the contract
- **b) Both parties are mistaken about the same term in the contract**
- c) One party is mistaken concerning facts in the contract
- d) None of the above

45.   Dan has just given you notice of his intention not to renew his tenancy, you go to the house and realise there is a lot of damage done to the property, you have not been to the house in over two years to inspect it and so you are not sure when the damage occurred, you have decided to bring a case against Dan for damages done to the house, **when does the Stature of Limitations run out on damage to property?**
- a) 1 year from the date you discover it
- b) 2 years from the date you discover it
- c) 3 years from the last date you inspected the property
- d) **6 years from the date the damage occurred**.

46.   The court ruled in the case of ***Hadley v Baxendale*** that:
- a) losses which arise naturally from the breach of contract.
- **b) losses which are in both parties contemplation which would probably arise from the breach.**
- c) losses which arise naturally from the breach of contract or which are in both parties contemplation as a probable result of its breach.
- d) losses which are reasonably foreseen by both parties at the time the contract is made are recoverable.

47.   Sam has worked for her employer for 3 years, she wants to leave her job, at the same time her employer is considering giving Sam notice to leave, her contract states that she and the employer must give the statutory minimum notice, advise Sam of the required notice she must give,
- e) One week

    **a) Two weeks**
    b) Four weeks
    c) Eight weeks

48. Which one of the following is not a remedy available where an employee wins a case for unfair dismissal?
    a) Compensation
    b) Re-instatement
    c) Re-engagement
    **d) Specific performance**

49. Which of the following statement are correct?
1) An employer is vicariously liable for the torts committed by employees in the course of their employment.
2) An employer is vicariously liable for the torts committed by their self-employed contractors in the course of their contracts.
    **a) 1 only**
    b) 2 only
    c) 1 and 2
    d) None

50. Which ONE of the following is normally implied into a contract of employment?
    a) The employer's duty to provide a reference
    b) The employees duty to follow all instructions
    c) The employer's duty to provide work
    **d) The employer's duty to pay wages**

## Solutions to Multiple Choice Questions

### Section Four – LO4 MCQs

1.    The case of **Rowland v Divall (1923)** defined was brought under which
Section 12(1)of the Sale of Goods and Supply of Services Act 1980
   a)    **Good title**
   b)    Fit for purpose
   c)    Merchantable quality
   d)    Fits the description

2.    The terms of the sale of Goods and Supply of Services are defined in the
   a)  Sale of goods and Supply of Services Act 1981
   b)  Sale of goods and Supply of Services Act 1990
   **c)  Sale of goods and Supply of Services Act 1980**
   d)  Sale of goods and Supply of Services Act 1880

3.    Under **Section 27 of the SGSSA 1980** if agreed, there is an obligation on the
seller to deliver the goods to the buyer.
   a)    **true**
   b)    false

4.    **Section 12(2) of the SGSSA 1980** states that:
   a)    The seller must inform the buyer of any incumbrances
   b)    The buyer must ask if there are any incumbrances
   **c)    There goods must be free from any incumbrances**
   d)    The goods can have an incumbrance so long as the buyer agrees
   to them at the time of purchase

5.     Stoppage in transit refers to:
   a)    The driver delivering the goods to the specified buyer must do so
   without stopping
   b)    The seller can stop the goods which have already been shipped
   to the buy should they become insolvent
   **c)    The goods can be stopped if the seller realises that the
   buyer cannot pay for them (gone into liquidation)**
   d)    The buyer can request that the goods can be stopped in transit,
   and be returned to the seller as they can't afford them.

6. The onus of proof in a claim for defective products is
   a) On the seller
   b) The manufacturer
   **c) The consumer**
   d) The public

7. The seller can only transfer such rights as they possess
   **a)     Yes, the seller can only transfer such rights as they possess**
   b)     Yes only if agreed by both parties at the time of the sale
   c)     No, the buyer has no right to possession unless transferred by the seller
   d)     No, only if the buyer can prove they bought it in good faith

8. Ownership passes when the contract is made, if:
   a)     the goods reached the buyer in a reasonable time
   b)     the goods were of satisfactory quality
   c)     the goods were as stated in the agreement
   **d)     if the goods are in a deliverable state**

9. If the goods are not in a deliverable state, ownership passes when:
   a)     the buyer informs the seller that the goods are not in a deliverable state
   **b)     when the goods have been put in such state, and the buyer has been informed**
   c)     when the goods are delivered
   d)     then the buyer asks for them to be delivered

10. If the goods must be weighed or measured by the seller, ownership passes once
   a)     the seller informs the buyer that they are the correct weight
   **b)     the goods have been weighed or measured and the seller informed**
   c)     the buy informs the seller they do not need the goods weighted any more
   d)     the seller makes an informed guess as to the weight of the goods

11. A defective product is one that
   a)     Has holes in it
   b)     Is not fit for purpose
   c)     One that is not merchantable quality
   **d)     Fails to provide safety which a person is entitled to expect**

12. Where the goods are sold *"on approval"* the ownership passes once the:
   a)     seller approved the deliver
   b)     seller crosses out the approval requirement on the contract

c)      buyer believes the seller when they said the goods were in good condition

**d)      when the buyer approves the goods and after a reasonable time.**

13.      If specific goods perish after a contract is made, but before delivery, the contract is:
     **a)      void**
     b)      voidable
     c)      unenforceable
     d)      frustrated

14.      What does 'nemo dat quod non habet' mean?
     a)      no one can give that which he has not got
     b)      seller cannot sell if they are under 18
     c)      the seller must confirm the weight and measurements
     **d)      no one can sell which he does not own**

15.      HACCP is the anagram for the
     a)      Hot and cold central point
     **b)      Hazard analysis and critical control points**
     c)      Hazard and critical control points
     d)      Hazard area control and chilled points

16.      What is the rules in regarding to sale prices
     a)      Advertised in the same store for one week previous
     **b)      Been advertised in any chain store for 28 days in the last three months**
     c)      Been advertised in the same store for 28 days in the last three months
     d)      Been advertised at a higher price for more than 28 days

17.      If a delivery time is agreed,
     a)      the delivery must be in a reasonable time
     **b)      time is assumed to be of the essence**
     c)      the delivery is implied to be within one day
     d)      time can be changed with the agreement of the seller and courier

18.      If the buyer fails to take delivery within a reasonable time they are:
     a)      entitled to return the goods to the buyer
     b)      have the goods at a cheaper price
     **c)      liable for any loss**
     d)      liable for the sellers restocking fees

19. If the price of the goods is not agreed at the time of delivery, the buy must
    pay:
    a) whatever price is on the invoice
    b) a reasonable price
    **c) a reasonable price depending on the market conditions and condition of the goods**
    d) the price which the buy believes they are worth

20. Misleading advertising is
    a) When a consumer is happy with the items as advertised on the radio
    **b) When a seller knowingly makes false claims**
    c) When the advertisement is for children's toys before 7pm
    d) A consumer wishes to make a seller have catalogues printed

21. The buyer may reject the entire delivery if the amount is more or less than agreed, however:
    **a) minute deviations won't apply**
    b) deviations must be within industry standards
    c) the seller can insist that the buyer take deliver
    d) the buyer can demand the seller come and take the extra away or bring more if the delivery is less than agreed

22. The function of the Competition and consumer Protection Agency
    a) To provide information to sellers to ensure they can get away with prohibited practices
    **b) To investigate sellers who are not adhering to the CPA 2007**
    c) To promote ways in which consumers can bring the sellers to the small claims court
    d) To keep an eye on prices so that sellers know their competitors markets

23. Buyers don't have to accept delivery by instalments unless;
    **a) previously agreed by both parties**
    b) the buyer was unsure if they wanted instalments at the time of purchase
    c) the seller contacted them and told them they were obliged to
    d) both parties believed the other would agree to it

24. The case of **Priest v Last** involved
    a) section 12 SGSSA 1980
    b) section 13 SGSSA 1980
    **c) section 14 SGSSA 1980**
    d) section 15 SGSSA 1980

25.  The buyer has no duty to return rejected goods
     **a) true**
     b)  false

26.  Prohibited practices are actions such as
     a)  Misappropriate claims
     **b) Aggressive practices**
     c)  Adamant claims
     d)  product development

27.  An agreement to prevent the right to examine goods is;
     a)  allowable on the agreement of both parties
     **b) not allowed under any circumstances**
     c)  allowed on the acceptance of the buyer
     d)  not allowed unless the court determines otherwise

28.  A buyer can sue for damages for breach of a condition or warranty, but;
     a)  can only reject the goods for a breach of a warranty
     b)  can only reject the goods for fraudulent misrepresentation
     **c) can only reject the goods for a breach of condition**
     d)  cannot reject the goods, but must instigate legal action

29.  An aggressive practice is one that
     **a) Entices a seller into a contract**
     b)  allows the buyers to decide freely their purchases
     c)  Allows sellers to provide false information
     d)  Misleads buyers as to the geographical origin or the goods

30.  A Lien is the seller's right to;
     **a) withhold delivery as long as they still have possession**
     b)  stop the goods in transit and have them returned
     c)  sue the buyer for non-acceptance
     d)  have the goods diverted to another buyer for resale

31.  The seller has a right to resell if the goods are perishable, or if notice is given;
     a)  when a buyer agrees to the resale
     **b) fails to pay within a reasonable time**
     c)  the seller gets higher offer from the new buyer
     d)  the seller believes the buyer cannot pay for the goods

32.  A misleading practice is one that
     a)  Helps consumers to identify lying sellers
     **b) Tells lies about how the product is made**
     c)  Gives accurate information about the product itself

d)      Mislead consumers as to where the goods are stored

33.   Market overt protects a buyer from any prosecution for the buying of encumbrance goods providing;
a)      the goods are bought on a market day
**b)      the goods are bought during the market official opening times**
c)      the goods are bought when the market stalls are set up regardless of the time
d)      the goods are bought from a market dealer.

34.   The Consumer Protection Act was enacted in
a)      1997
b)      2008
**c)      2007**
d)      1999

35.   The Sale of Goods and Supply of Services Act 1980 is a:
**a) prospective act**
b) retrospective act
c) perspective act
d) nominal act.

36.   Under the Sale of Goods and Supply of Services Act 1980 the term implied into the contract that the supplier will carry out the service with reasonable case and skills is treated as a:
a)      Condition.
**b)      Warranty.**
c)      Innominate term.
d)      Representation

37.   Susie bought a bike from "Best Bikes Ltd" telling the sales assistant that she knew nothing about bikes but wanted a bike suitable for riding on rough terrain. She bought the bike which was recommended to her by the assistant, however, although the bike was fine around town, the wheels and frame bent the first time she used it on rough terrain. Her action against "Best Bikes Ltd" would be for breach of which section of the Sale of Goods Act 1980?
a)      12
b)      13
**c)      14**
d)      15

38.   When do goods not have to be of a reasonable standard according to **S.14 of the SGSSA 1980**?
a)      Second hand goods

b) Goods on sale
**c) Issues brought to the attention of the buyer before the sale**
d) They goods a bought online

39. A contract for the sale of goods is one where:
a) A seller gives goods to another by way of a contract, for safe keeping
b) Goods are passed to another to use in his business
**c) A seller transfers or agrees to transfer, the property in goods to the buyer for a money consideration called the price**
d) Goods are loaned under a contract of hire to a customer

40. What type of goods are not covered under the **Sale of Goods and Supply of Services Act 1980**
a) Cars
b) Automobiles
c) Crops from land for sale
**d) Land**

41. Where the transfer of the goods is to take place at a future time, this contract is called:
a) sale
**b) an agreement to sell.**
c) provisional sale
d) conditional sale

42. In a sales contract, a breach of a <u>condition</u> gives the aggrieved party right to:
a) repudiate the contract
b) claim damages
**c) repudiate the contract and also claim damages**
d) none of the above

43. In a sales contract, a breach of a <u>warranty</u> gives the aggrieved party right to:
a) repudiate the contract
**b) claim damages**
c) repudiate the contract and also claim damages
d) none of the above

44. The maxim is *"nemo det quod non habet"* which means that:
a) no one is an owner unless he pays for the goods
**b) no one can give what he has not got**
c) the sale of goods must be in writing
d) none of the above

45.    A contract of sale of goods is a contract whereby the seller transfers or agrees to transfer the property:
   a)   agreement to sell for a price
   b)   an agreement to swap
   **c)   in goods to the buyer for a price**
   d)   none of the above

46.    A contract of sale of goods may be made:
   a)   in writing
   b)   orally,
   c)   may be implied from the conduct of the parties.
   **d)   all of the above**

47.    In a contract for sale of goods, they buyer may have an action, in respect of physical injuries caused by defect in the goods;
   a)   against the manufacturer
   b)   against the seller
   c)   against the seller and also the manufacturer
   **d)   all of the above**

48.    For the purpose of consumer law, which act defines a consumer;
   a) The Consumer Protection Act 2007
   b) Safety, health and Welfare at Work Act, 2005
   c) The Sale of Goods Act 1983
   **d) The Sale of Goods and Supply of Services Act 1980**

49.    A Condition is a stipulation which is:
   a) important
   b) unimportant
   **c) goes to the heart of the contract**
   d) gives the parties the power to choose importance

50.    A contract for the sale of goods includes
   a) sale only
   b) agreement to sell only
   c) sale and agreement to sell
   **d) all of the above**

## Solutions to Multiple Choice Questions

**Section Five – LO5 MCQs**

1.     How many parties are there to a "Promissory note" and a "bill of exchange"?
       a)     There are three parties to a "Promissory note" and three to a "bill of exchange"
       b)     There are five parties to a "Promissory note" and two to a "bill of exchange
       c)     There is one party to a "Promissory note" and three to a "bill of exchange"
       **d)     There are two parties to a "Promissory note and three to a bill of exchange"**

2.     Where a cheque has been issued, and there is a discrepicancy between the amount in words and figures, which shall be paid
       a) the amount in figures
       **b) the amount written in words**
       c) the cheque is void
       d) none of the above.

3.     'Negotiable' means transferable. In the case of a negotiable instrument Negotiation can take place from one person to another:
       a)   by mere delivery or by endorsement and delivery.
       **b)   only by endorsement and delivery to the drawee**
       c)   delivery is not negotiation
       d)   none of the above

4.     Money orders; Postal orders and Share certificates; are examples of:
       **a)   Negotiable Instruments**
       b)   Non-negotiable instruments
       c)   A mix of Negotiable and Non- Negotiable Instruments
       d)   None of the above

5.     A Bill of Exchange, when it is not payable on demand, is entitled to get:
       a)   3 days grace period.
       b)   10 days grace period
       c)   the day of maturity only
       **d)   none of the above**

6. Where a negotiable instrument is dishonoured, notice is given to:
   a) drawer only
   b) all previous endorsees.
   **c) drawer and all previous endorsees.**
   d) none of the above

7. The undertaking contained in a promissory note, to pay a certain sum of money is
   a) conditional
   **b) unconditional**
   c) may be conditional or unconditional depending upon the circumstances
   d) none of the above.

8. A bill of exchange contains a/an
   a) unconditional undertaking
   **b) unconditional order**
   c) conditional undertaking
   d) conditional order.

9. A Cheque is a
   a) promissory note
   **b) bill of exchange**
   c) both (a) and (b) above
   d) None of the above.

10. A promissory note or bill of exchange which is not expressed to be payable on demand, at sight or on presentment is at maturity
    a) on the 30th day after the day on which it is expressed to be payable
    **b) on the 3rd day after the day on which it is expressed to be payable**
    c) on the 5th day after the day on which it is expressed to be payable
    d) on the 4th day after the day on which it is expressed to be payable.

11. In a promissory note, the amount of money payable
    **a) must be certain**
    b) may be certain or uncertain
    c) is usually uncertain
    d) none of the above.

12. A bill is drawn payable to 'A' or order. 'A' indorses it to 'B', the indorsement not containing the words '"or order" or any equivalent words. Can 'B' negotiate the instrument?
    **a) yes**
    b) no
    c) not always

d) none of the above

13. The endorsement of a negotiable instrument followed by delivery
a) transfers to the endorsee the property in the bill, provided the endorsement must be an endorsement in full
b) does not transfer the property in the bill to anyone
**c) transfers to the endorsee the property in the bill**
d) transfers to the holder the property in bill.

14. If the words "not negotiable" are used with special crossing in a cheque, the cheque is
**a) not transferable**
b) transferable
c) negotiable under certain circumstances
d) none of the above.

15. Crossing of a cheque effects the
**a) negotiability of the cheque**
b) mode of payment on the cheque
c) both (a) and (b)
d) none of the above.

16. Dishonour by non-acceptance takes place
a) when the bill is properly presented for acceptance, except where presentment is excused, but the drawee makes the default in accepting it
b) when the Bill is properly presented for acceptance, except where presentment is excused, but the drawee makes the default in paying it
**c) when the bill is properly presented for payment, except where presentment is excused, but the drawee fails to accept it**
d) none of the above.

17. When a cheque has become invalid because of the expiry of the stipulated period, can it be re-validated by the drawer by alteration of dates?
a) yes, the drawer can re-validate the cheque by alteration of dates
b) no, the drawer cannot re-validate it by so alteration of dates
**c) although the drawer cannot revalidate the cheque, but the drawee can at his discretion reissue it**
d) none of the above.

18. A protest must contain
a) the name of the person for whom the instrument has been protested
b) the name of the person against whom the instrument has been protested
c) the instrument itself or its literal transcript

**d) all of the above.**

19. A protest is made by
    a) the drawer
    b) the endorser
    **c) a notary**
    d) none of the above.

20. Where a cheque is crossed generally the banker on whom it is drawn
    a) shall not pay it otherwise than to a banker
    b) shall not pay it otherwise than to the holder
    c) shall not pay it to a banker
    d) none of the above.

## Solutions to Multiple Choice Questions

Section Six – LO6 MCQs

1.  Sources of company law
    **a) Company law Legislation,**
    b)  Case law and Precedent
    c)  EU law
    d)  Code of Ethics

2.  A Public company can
    **a) Sell shares on stock market,**
    b)  Can't sell shares on the open market
    c)  Transfer shares by deed
    d)  Swap shares

3.  A Private company
    **a) Can't sell shares to public (only transfer),**
    b)  Can sell shares to the public
    c)  Sell shares at their annual general meeting
    d)  None of the above

4.  When a company is limited by shares it's
    **a) Shareholders' liability is limited to their investments**
    b)  Shareholders are liable for all losses
    c)  Shareholders are liable for all losses which they were aware the company were making
    d)  Shareholders are jointly and liable for losses which stem from their involvement in the decisions

5.  The Doctrine of a Separate legal personality
    **a) A company is a legal person separate and distinct from its members - can enter contracts, be sued, own assets**
    b)  A company is a NOT legal person separate and distinct from its members. The directors own the company
    c)  A company is not liable for contracts its directors enter on their behalf

6.  The Doctrine of Ultra Vires occurs
    a)  When a company enters contracts which they have the power to do
    **b) When a company enters a contract which they do not have the power to do**
    c)  When a director employs a shadow director

d) When the shareholders agree on directs remuneration

7. The Director Manages the Company on behalf of shareholders
   **a) True**
   b) False

8. Which is the most common type of registered company?
   a) An unlimited company
   b) A company limited by guarantee
   **c) A private company limited by shares**
   d) A public limited company

9. A sole trader's liability for debts incurred in the course of business is limited to the value of business assets.
   a) True
   **b) False**

10. Which of the following is not a type of capital?
    a) Allotted capital
    b) Paid up capital
    **c) Debenture capital**
    d) Issued capital

11. Which of the following does not describe the nature of a floating charge?
    a) It is a charge over a class of assets both present and future book debts
    **b) It is a charge over a class of asset which, in the ordinary course of business, changes from time to time**
    c) It is a charge that requires the company to obtain consent if it wishes to deal with the charged asset in the ordinary course of business.
    d) It is a charge over stock in trade, raw material and finished articles

12. Which of the following statements describes the decision of the House of Lords in **Salomon v Salomon & Co Ltd (1897)?**
    a) A company has unlimited liability for its debts
    b) A company cannot issue floating charges to its members
    **c) A company is a legal entity, distinct from its members**
    d) A single member cannot form a company

13. Which of the following statements is not a correct proposition in relation to the role of a promoter of a company?
    a) A person who takes the necessary steps to form a company
    b) A person who owes fiduciary duties to a company

c) A person who is acts as a director of a company during the course of the promotion of the company

**d) A person who can become a member of a company on incorporation of the company**

14. Which body exercises the control of a registered company?
    e) The general meeting
    **a) The board of directors**
    b) The company secretary
    c) The general meeting and the board of directors

15. Which of the following describes a director with day to day responsibility for a company and its board of directors?
    a) Chairman
    b) Finance Director
    c) President
    **d) Managing director**

16. Which of the following is not a true statement relating to the nature and scope of fraudulent trading as contained in Companies Act 2014?
    a) In the course of the winding up, it appears that any business of the company has been carried on with intent to defraud creditors of the company or for any fraudulent purpose.
    b) The liquidator can apply to the court for a declaration that any persons who were knowingly parties to the carrying on of the business in this way be liable to make such contributions to the company's assets as the court thinks proper.
    c) Fraudulent trading means conduct that is Knowingly and intentionally dishonest according to the notions of ordinary decent business people.
    **d) Only directors or officers of the company can have action taken against them**

17. The Minimum number of members in case of private company is
    **a) 1**
    b) 2
    c) 3
    d) 4

18. Liability of a member in case of a private company is
    **a) Limited**
    b) Unlimited
    c) Both (a) or (b)
    d) None of the above

19.    Maximum no. of persons in case of partnership banking business
_____
   **a) 10**
   b) 20
   c) 30
   d) 5

20.    Minimum paid up share capital in case of a DAC is _____
   a) 10%
   b) 100%
   **c) 25%**
   d) 50%

21.    Minimum no. of Directors in case of a LTD is _____
   **a) 1**
   b) 2
   c) 3
   d) 4

22.    Minimum no. of Directors in case of DAC is _____
   a) 1
   **b) 2**
   c) 3
   d) 4

23.    Transfer of shares in the partnership firm is
   a) Restricted
   b) Freely transferable
   c)  Prohibited
   **d) None of the above**

24.    Generally Company liability is
   **a) Limited**
   b) Unlimited
   c) Unlimited by shares
   d) None of the above

25.    The companies which are formed under special Act. Those companies are known as
   a) Chartered companies
   **b) Statutory companies**
   c) Registered companies
   d) None of these

26.    The companies which are formed under Companies Act. 2014. They will be known as

a) Chartered companies
b) Statutory companies
**c) Registered companies**
d) None of these

27. Transfer of shares in the case of public company is
a) Prohibited
b) Restricted
**c) Freely transferable**
d) None of these

28. Private company can start its business immediately after the issue of

a) Certificate of commencement
**b) Certificate of Incorporation**
c) Both of the above
d) None of the above

29. Public company should start business only after getting certificate of
a) Incorporation
**b) Trading Certificate**
c) Commencement certificate
d) All of the above

30. A company can change its name at its own discretion by passing _____
a) Ordinary resolution
**b) Special resolution**
c) Boards resolution
d) None of the above

## Solutions to Multiple Choice Questions

Section Seven – LO7 MCQs

1. When the auditor has reason to believe an illegal act has occurred, they should:
   a) inquire of management at a level above, those likely to be involved with the illegality.
   b) consider accumulating additional evidence to determine if there is actually an illegal act.
   c) consult with the client's legal advisors.
   **d) all of the above**

2. If the auditor believes that the financial statements are not fairly stated or if they are unable to reach a conclusion because of insufficient evidence, the auditor:
   a) should withdraw from the engagement.
   b) should request an increase in audit fees so that more resources can be used to conduct the audit.
   **c) has the responsibility of notifying financial statement users through the auditor's report.**
   d) report the client to the audit committee

3. The responsibility for adopting sound accounting policies and maintaining adequate internal controls in accounting practices is the responsibility of the:
   a) board of directors.
   **b) company management.**
   c) financial statement auditor.
   d) company's internal audit department

4. The responsibility of the presentation of a fair and accurate financial statement lies jointly with the management and the auditors,
   a) true
   **b) false**

5. Which of the following statements is most correct regarding errors and fraud?
   **a) an error is unintentional, whereas fraud is intentional.**
   b) frauds occur more often than errors in financial statements.
   c) errors are always fraud and frauds are always errors.
   d) auditors have more responsibility for detecting fraud than correcting it

6. Where an auditor uncovers fraud by management which was unintentional and accidental, this leaves them unaccountable for any fraudulent activity,?
    a) true
    **b) false**

7. Which of the following is the auditor least likely to do when aware of an illegal act?
    a) discuss the matter with the client's legal advisors
    b) obtain evidence about the potential effect of the illegal act on the financial statements.
    **c) contact the Gardaí regarding potential legal consequences**
    d) report the matter to the inland revenue

8. An auditor must not assume their client in inherently dishonest, however they must consider that this is a possibility, this would be classed as:
    a) unprofessional behaviour.
    **b) an attitude of professional scepticism.**
    c) due diligence.
    d) a rule in the IFAC's Code of Professional Conduct

9. If a number of employees decided amongst themselves to perpetrate fraud in the accounting, would this be a relatively easy for the auditor to detect?
    a) yes
    **b) no**

10.    The difference between an accountant and an auditor is, the accountant must possess the standards a reasonable accountant, and apply this knowledge to producing the financial statements of a company. Whereas the auditor must be an expert accountant giving them the knowledge and experience so that they can assess the standards of accounting and make an informed decision about the accuracy of the financial statements.
    **a) true**
    b) false

Contract law list of cases and rulings
**Clifton v Palumbo**
**Summary**_____
**Ruling** = the wording "prepared to offer" was not deemed to be adequately clear or detailed to be defined as an offer.

**Gibson v Manchester City Council**
**Summary**_____
**Ruling** = the wording "may be prepared to sell" was not deemed to be not adequately certain to be defined as an offer.

**Advertisements**
**Grainger & Sons v Gough**
**Summary**_____
**Ruling** = Advertisements are generally classed as invitations to treat

**Carlill v Carbolic Smokeball Company**
**Summary**_____
**Ruling** = the defendants lodgement of £1000 into their bank account was defined as a clear intention to be bound (unilateral offer)

**Display of goods**
**Fisher v Bell**
**Summary**_____
**Ruling** = Display of goods are generally classed as invitations to treat

**Pharmaceutical Society of Great Britain v Boots Cash Chemist**
**Summary**_____
**Ruling** = Display of goods are generally classed as invitations to treat

**Auctions**
**Harris v Nickerson**
**Summary**_____
**Ruling** = Adverts are generally classed as invitations to treat

**Barry v Davies**
**Summary**_____
**Ruling** =  The auctioneer cannot reject highest bidder

**Tenders**
**Spencer v Harding**
**Summary**_____
**Ruling** =  Tenders are generally invitations to treat, there is no obligation to sell to highest bidder.

**Harvela Investments v Royal Trust Co of Canada**

**Summary**_____

**Ruling =** Tenders are generally invitations to treat, the seller cannot accept referential bidding, as a price must be certain.

## Rejection/termination of offer/counteroffer
**Hyde v Wrench**
**Summary**_____

**Ruling =** A counter offer amounts to a rejection and therefore a termination of the original offer.

## Tinn v Hoffman
**Summary**_____

**Ruling =** The offer was for 1200 tonnes and the defendant ordered 800 tonnes, this was deemed a counter offer and rejection of the original and termination of the offer

## Silence not a form of acceptance
**Felthouse v Bindley**
**Summary**_____

**Ruling =** an offer cannot be accepted by silence, the offerer saying if I hear no more from you then...... is not an acceptable form of acceptance

## Communication of acceptance in Unilateral Contracts
**Carlill v Carbolic Smoke Ball**
**Summary**_____

**Ruling =** Unilateral contracts are accepted by performance

## Acceptance by post
**Adams v Lindsell**
**Summary**_____

**Ruling =** Acceptance is effective when the letter is posted

## Consideration
**Thomas –v- Thomas**
**Summary**_____

**Ruling =** Consideration must be sufficient, but need not be adequate

## Chappell v Nestle
**Summary**_____

**Ruling =** The wrappers from bars were good consideration

## Performance of a duty imposed by the general law not sufficient unless something over and above that public duty
**Glasbrook Bros v-Glamorgan**
**Summary**_____

**Ruling =** Performance of existing contractual duty not sufficient

### Stilk v Myrick
**Summary**_____
**Ruling =** A promise to get extra consideration for a pre-existing duty is **NOT** good consideration

### Hartley v Ponsonby
**Summary**_____
**Ruling =** A promise to get extra consideration for going OVER the existing duty **IS** good consideration

### Part payment of a debt is insufficient
### The Rule in Pinnel's Case
**Summary**_____
**Ruling =** part payment of a debt is not good consideration, the debt is still owed, EXCEPTION= where a third party makes the payment of behalf of the person owing the debt

### Must not be "past" consideration
### Re McArdle
**Summary**_____
**Ruling =** A defendant cannot get payment for a fee that is agreed after the work is already started or completed
### Consideration must move from promisee (not third party)
### Tweddle –v- Atkinson
**Summary**_____
**Ruling =** The consideration must move from the promise, not a third party, (i.e. someone else paying your bill)

### Intentions to Create Legal Relations
- family, domestic or social (no intention)
- commercial (intention exists).

*Both rebuttable (prove otherwise, proven not true or not the case) based on each cases merits*

### Family, Domestic or Social
### Balfour –v- Balfour
**Summary**_____
**Ruling =** There is a presumption that no intention between husband and wife

### Merritt v Merritt
**Summary**_____
**Ruling =** There is an intention where the parties signed an agreement that it is binding

**Parent and child**
**Jones –v- Padavatton**
**Summary**_____
**Ruling =** There is no intention to create legal relations between parents and children

**Edwards v Skyways**
**Summary: The Defendant was promised a bonus payment, described as 'ex gratia', he had relied upon the promise in accepting a redundancy package, but the employer stated there was no intention to create legal relations as the term ex gratia was used to avoid paying taxes and therefore not legally binding on them.**
**Ruling =** this was a commercial agreement, there was a meeting where the courts described the meeting "meeting of minds", where the terms were agreed. The court held that there was an intention to create legal relations, they were his employers, it did not matter what the wording of that agreement was.
*It is possible to rebut presumptions, if the parties can show evidence that legal relations were intended, this would depend on the degree of closeness and how much the parties relied on the intention to create legal relations*

**Commercial agreements are implied to have the intention to create legal relations**
**Rose and Frank v Crompton**
**Summary**_____
**Ruling =** Where a company inserts an honour clause or exemption clause into a contract the presumption of intention can be rebutted.

**Capacity**
**Minors**
**Nash –v- Inman**
**Summary**_____
**Ruling =** Contracts for necessaries and beneficial services are binding on minors

**Chapple v Cooper**
**Summary**_____
**Ruling =** Contracts for necessaries and beneficial services are binding on minors

**Privity of Contract**
**Tweddle –v- Atkinson**
**Summary**_____

**Ruling =** This is the rule that a person who was not a party to the contract cannot enforce the terms of that contract, nor can those terms be enforced against that person.

Exception = if the third party is a beneficiary under the contract, i.e. married women, children under health insurance policies of parents

**List of cases in tort**

**Vicarious Liability:**
Moynihan v Moynihan:
McKenna V Best Travel
**Summary**_____
**Ruling =**

**Trespass to the Person:**
Scott v Shephard:
**Summary**_____
**Ruling =**

**Battery:**
Cole v Turner:
R v Cotesworth:
**Summary**_____
**Ruling =**

**Assault:**
Stephens v Myers:
R v Ireland:
**Summary**_____
**Ruling =**

**False Imprisonment:**
Brid v Jones:
Hearing v Boyle:
**Summary**_____
**Ruling =**

**Defences:**
**Self Defence:**
Cregan v O'Sullivan:
**Summary**_____
**Ruling =**

**Consent:**
**Summary**_____
**Ruling =**
**Necessity:**
Lawful Authority:
**Summary**_____
**Ruling =**

**Trespass to Goods:**

Farrell v Minister for Agri & Food:
**Summary**_____
**Ruling =**

**Detinue:**
Poole v Burns:
**Summary**_____
**Ruling =**

**Conversion:**
Hollins v Fowler:
**Summary**_____
**Ruling =**

**Trespass to Land:**
O'Brien v McNamee:
Whelan v Madigan:
**Summary**_____
**Ruling =**

**Remedies:**
Re-entry, Ejectment, Mesne Profits and Damages. Injunctions in relation to a continuing trespass.
**Summary**_____
**Ruling =**

**Defences:**
Consent, Lawful Authority.
**Summary**_____
**Ruling =**

**Necessity:**
Cope v Sharpe:
**Summary**_____
**Ruling =**

**Strict Liability**
Rylands v Fletcher:
**Summary**_____
**Ruling =**

**Nuisance:**
Connolly v South of Ireland Asphalt Co:
**Summary**_____
**Ruling =**

**Defence to nuisance**
Sturges v Brideman:
**Summary**_____
**Ruling =**


**Consent:**
Thomas v Lewis:
**Summary**_____
**Ruling =**


**Public Nuisance:**
Mullar v Foster:
Cunningham v McGrath Brothers:
**Summary**_____
**Ruling =**


**Passing Off:**
Polycell Products Ltd v O'Carroll & Ors:
McCambridge ltd v Joseph Brennan Bakeries: 2012: SCt:
**Summary**_____
**Ruling =**


**Goodwill?**
An Post v Irish Permanent:
DSG Retail v PC World:
**Summary**_____
**Ruling =**


**Misrepresentation/Confusion?**
Jameson v Irish Distillers:
Jiff lemon case:
**Summary**_____
**Ruling =**


**Damage:**
Falcon Travel v Owners Abroad Group:
**Summary**_____
**Ruling =**


**Negligence: Define** _____
**Duty of Care**
Donoghue Stephenson
Kirby v Burke & Holloway
Hedley Byrne v Heller
Anns v Merton London Borough Council
Caparo Industries v Dickman

Glencar v Mayo Co Co
**Summary**_____
**Ruling =**

**Standard of care:**
Haley v London Electricity Board:
**Summary**_____
**Ruling =**

**Causation:**
Kenny v O'Rourke:
**Summary**_____
**Ruling =**

**MATERIAL CONTRIBUTION TEST:**
McGhee v National Coal Board:
Quinn v Midwestern Health Board:
Skull rule and remoteness of damage.
Breslin & Corcoran & MIBI:
**Summary**_____
**Ruling =**

**Remoteness of Damage:**
Re Polemis:
Condon v CIS:
**Summary**_____
**Ruling =**

**Egg Shell Skull Rule:**
Smith v Leech Brain & Co Ltd:
**Summary**_____
**Ruling =**

**Res Ipsa Loquitor:**
Scott v London St Katherine Docks Co:
**Summary**_____
**Ruling =**

**Pure Economic Loss:**
Hedley Byrne v Heller:
Ward v McMaster:
**Summary**_____
**Ruling =**

**Professional Negligence:**
Dunne v The National Maternity Hospital:

**Summary**_____
**Ruling =**

**Solicitors' Negligence:**
Roche v Peilow:
**Summary**_____
**Ruling =**

**Defamation:**
Quigley v Creation:
Speight V Gosnay
**Summary**_____
**Ruling =**

**Defamation**
Berry v Irish Times:
Reynolds v Malocco:
Reynolds v Times Newspapers:
Talbot v Hermitage Golf club:
**Summary**_____
**Ruling =**

**Occupiers Liability:**
Power v Governor of Cork Prison:
**Summary**_____
**Ruling =**

**Product Liability:**
O'Byrne v Gloucester & Ors:
**Summary**_____
**Ruling =**

**Employer's Liability:**
Connolly v Dundalk UDC & Mahon & Philips:
**Summary**_____
**Ruling =**

**Standard of Care:**
Harris v Bright Asphalt:
**Summary**_____
**Ruling =**

**Limitation of Actions:**
Statute of Limitations – 6 years for tort (assault, battery, trespass, etc.) from date on which cause of action accrued- BUT now 2 years for personal injury
Defamation - 1 year

Devlin v Roche:
**Summary**_____
**Ruling =**

## Undiscovered property damage? (statute of limitations)
O'Donnell v Kilsaran Concrete Ltd:
**Summary**_____
**Ruling =**

# CPA/ACCA/ATI - BUSINESS LAW CRAM NOTES

***Here's wishing you the best of luck in your exams. You can pop onto my webpage at www.teresaclyne.com for further information.***

*If you have any queries on this booklet you can contact me by email on teresaclyne@mail.com*